Penguin Books
Protecting Your Hom

Chris Gill has spent virtually the whole of his working life researching, writing and editing magazines and books to help the consumer. After training as an engineer, he joined Consumers' Association in 1972 as a researcher and writer on do-it-yourself subjects for *Which?* magazine. In 1985 he left to set up Fox + Partners, a consultancy dealing in every aspect of information, from microcomputer database systems through technical writing and editing to graphic design. His interest in home security goes back to 1982, when his London house was burgled twice in six months. He now lives near Bath with his wife and baby.

Founded in 1797, **Norwich Union** is one of the country's leading household insurers, providing cover for more than 1 million homes throughout the UK. The company therefore has a vested interest in home security, which is why it offers premium discounts to policy-holders who take specified precautionary measures.

Besides insuring people and their property, Norwich Union offers a wide range of financial services, including endowment mortgage policies, pensions and other investment plans. The assets of the group amount to well over £10,000 million.

Protecting Your Home
The Norwich Union Guide

Chris Gill

Penguin Books

PENGUIN BOOKS

Published by the Penguin Group
27 Wrights Lane, London W8 5TZ, England
Viking Penguin Inc., 40 West 23rd Street, New York, New York 10010, USA
Penguin Books Australia Ltd, Ringwood, Victoria, Australia
Penguin Books Canada Ltd, 2801 John Street, Markham, Ontario, Canada LR3 1B4
Penguin Books (NZ) Ltd, 182–190 Wairau Road, Auckland 10, New Zealand

Penguin Books Ltd, Registered Offices: Harmondsworth, Middlesex, England

First published 1988

Typeset by Fox + Partners, Bath, and PCS, Frome
Illustrations (not otherwise credited) by Tom Cross, Bristol

Made and printed in Great Britain by Richard Clay Ltd, Bungay

Contents

Acknowledgements

The creation of this book has been a team effort, and although I take responsibility for what the book says, much of the credit for its existence and for any merit it possesses must go to my old friend and colleague Kathryn Deane — like me, a graduate of *Handyman Which?*.

Thanks are due to the many manufacturers of home security equipment and other goods which are described in these pages – in particular to Yale and J E Reynolds (makers of ERA locks and fittings) for providing many of the illustrations; to those members of the County of Avon Fire Brigade, Suffolk Fire Service and Suffolk Constabulary who read the proofs of the book and made helpful comments on them; and not least to those within Norwich Union who have helped in various ways.

By sponsoring the book, Norwich Union have allowed us to devote more resources to its preparation than would otherwise have been possible; if the book strikes you as good value, you have them to thank — particularly Ken Hurst, Public Relations and Publicity Manager, and the Fire Society's General Management, who were quick to see the value of the project to their customers and to the public at large.

I am also grateful to the staff of the Personal Insurance and Claims areas of Norwich Union, who made very helpful comments on the proofs. But the opinions expressed in this book are my own, and not those of Norwich Union who, while supporting this book wholeheartedly, have given me complete freedom in writing it.

1
Who needs security?

If you read this book and act upon it, your home will be safer than before (and much safer than most people's homes) from the threat of burglary. As a result, you will be largely relieved of a nagging worry that most householders share to some degree. But peace of mind comes only at the end of the process; before things can get better, they have to get worse.

You may be reading this book for the compelling reason that you have recently suffered a burglary. What has always seemed a rather remote and vague threat has suddenly become very real. If so, you have the advantage of powerful motivation to embark on the unattractive process of improving the security of your home. For most people, a burglary is a sufficiently shocking invasion of privacy to trigger a sharp reaction — a desire to do everything possible to prevent a repetition.

What you will want to know is what action to take, and you may as well skip the rest of this chapter and start reading the later ones that will give you the answers you need. But be warned: making a house secure is a painstaking business, and once the damage to your household is made good you may lose momentum as your fears fade along with the memory. You may need to remind yourself occasionally of just how saddened or outraged you feel right now.

If you have so far escaped burglary, motivation is more of a problem. You could gain it the hard way: close this book now, and wait until you are burgled (possibly not all that long to wait, if the figures quoted below are anything to go by). The less painful way is to read the rest of this chapter. It should give you the impetus you need to carry through the necessary security improvements to your home before you join the statistics.

You probably do not like to think about how vulnerable your home is to crime. You are not alone. We would all prefer to live in a world where crime wasn't a threat, and where homes didn't need the locks and bars of a prison. Dream if you like, but don't kid yourself that you actually live in such a world. More to the point, perhaps, don't kid yourself that your household is different from others, and immune from the general threat of a break-in. It's tempting; on page 12 are five ready-made excuses for not taking the threat of burglary seriously. But excuses are all they are, as you can see.

It is only by accepting and understanding the threat you face that you stand a chance of gaining the security — and the sense of security — that this book can offer you. As you read through the following chapters, you will become more and more aware of just how poorly protected your home is — but also of how you can go about putting things right.

How common is burglary?

The spectre of 'soaring crime statistics' is a great sales aid for makers of locks, latches and more expensive home security devices. It is not all sales talk: the number of burglaries generally does go up year after year. But there are problems in working out what the figures really mean. The official statistics necessarily cover only *reported* crimes. A steep increase in the rates could mean a steep increase in the number of burglaries — or it could just mean that a greater proportion of those that do happen are coming to the attention of the police. On the other hand, the figures clearly do not tell the whole story: many thefts are committed that are not reported, and so are not included in the official figures.

But the key points which emerge from a study of the available evidence are that:

• in 1986 (actually April '86 to March '87) reported domestic burglaries topped half a million — meaning that something like one in 35 homes reported a burglary

• taking into account estimates of unreported incidents, the chance of being burgled in a year may be as high as one in 25

● although the number of reported incidents does go up each year, the rate of increase is dropping significantly — between 1980 and 1983, the increase was a massive 46 per cent; between 1983 and 1986, it was a much lower 17 per cent.

But 'average' figures tell only part of the story. To get a closer approximation to *your* chances of being burgled, you need to take account of your own circumstances. The evidence suggests that:

● city properties suffer about twice the average rate of burglary, country places about half the average

● flats, maisonettes, houses isolated from others and those set back from the road, and affluent-looking homes are all more likely than average to be burgled

● there is probably little to choose between terraced, detached or semi-detached houses in similar settings.

Roughly speaking, the figures and estimates suggest that a city-centre flat might have a one-in-ten chance of being burgled in a year (or to put it another way, an even chance of being burgled in a period of five years); an estate house in a rural area might present only a fifth of the risk.

What's the damage?

You may take some comfort from the fact that, financially, most people lose relatively little when they suffer a burglary. The value of property stolen is often less than £100, and in a surprising number of cases nothing at all is taken. Over all domestic burglaries, the average loss is around £600 — a modest sum compared with the £18,000 that is the average value of the house contents. Break-in damage is not likely to be great, and any mess is more likely to result from the burglar's haste than from deliberate vandalism.

But for many people burglary has a more serious result: a deep sense of personal invasion following the realization that a criminal stranger has gone through your possessions. And the loss of property is not felt only in a financial sense — many possessions have great sentimental value; such possessions are irreplaceable, and there is almost no chance of getting them back again.

Five favourite fallacies

I'm all right — I'm insured
- are you *sure?* — read chapter 11 and find out why you might not be as well protected as you think
- you can't insure against the psychological damage you may suffer — in many cases, more important than the financial loss
- insurance won't bring back your treasured heirlooms and other possessions of sentimental value
- insurance won't pay for all the hassle involved in putting your home back together

I've nothing worth stealing
- it's probably untrue — no radios, watches or cash?
- even if it were true, how do you expect a burglar to know that?

A determined thief will get in anyway
- quite likely; but the point is that most thieves are not determined to rob you in particular — make it difficult, and they may well be put off

I'm only a tenant here
- you probably have almost as much to lose as an owner-occupier — and therefore almost as much to gain from improved security
- the owners may be just as interested as you in preventing a break-in — so don't assume that you will have to bear the whole cost of improved security yourself

Our dog will see off any intruder
- maybe, if your dog is highly aggressive or highly trained; but burglars are cleverer than dogs, and may be quite capable of coping with yours

Is improved security worthwhile?

There is little doubt that good security devices do cut the risk of being burgled, though there is a great deal of room for debate over how much. Some estimates suggest that in 1986 they prevented as many as 200,000 burglaries — almost half the number of actual ones.

Some security measures cost nothing — apart from a small investment of time. If you can develop a greater awareness of what is going on around you, and accept the fact that a burglary could happen to *you*, there are many ways in which you can reduce the risk of burglary without spending a penny. This book explains all these 'free' measures.

But locks, burglar alarms, and other security devices will of course cost you money. The checklist at the end of Chapter 2 gives some rough figures for the cost of improving various aspects of security, and Chapter 13 gives typical prices for individual items of security equipment. But in a nutshell: high-security door and window locks for a typical house would cost under £150 if you installed them yourself (and perhaps under £100); expect to pay perhaps the same again for professional installation. You can of course spend much larger amounts, particularly on complex alarm systems.

Proper security devices won't *guarantee* your security; conversely, the lack of them doesn't automatically mean that you *will* be burgled. If you are properly insured, a burglary might involve you in only incidental expense — perhaps a day off work while you get your house in order and convey the facts to the police and your insurers.

Some insurers offer discounts on the cost of insurance if your house is properly secured – but that alone is unlikely to be an adequate incentive: you could take a dozen years or more to recoup the cost of expensive locks and alarms from savings on lower insurance premiums. And, as Chapter 11 points out, you might be able to save more simply by switching to another insurance company.

So it is impossible to be sure that buying security devices — even relatively cheap ones — will yield a financial return. But weigh up all the other factors involved in burglary:

- the loss of irreplaceable personal possessions
- the psychological damage to you and your family
- the time and effort involved in making good the damage
- the consumption of police resources (which you pay for in one way or another).

In many eyes, the slightest reduction in the risk of suffering these burdens is enough to justify the cost of modest home security improvements — an expenditure which is likely to amount to no more than a small fraction of one per cent of the value of your home.

2
'Casing' your own property

Before you can strengthen your defences, you have to spot their
weaknesses; you then have to work out what improvements are
desirable and practicable. In both these tasks you may need
help, and it is not difficult to find. Of the few things in life that
are free, a visit from an expert consultant in home security,
perhaps surprisingly, is one. There is such a consultant — called
a Crime Prevention Officer (CPO) — attached to every police
force, and your local police station will be able to put you in
touch with the one for your area.

Your CPO should be a fount of advice on how to make your
home safer. But there is a lot of sense in taking a careful look at
your home from the security point of view before the CPO's
visit. You will then be able to make the best use of the CPO's
time, and make sure that your own circumstances and special
problems have been taken into account. If you are in a position
to discuss your security needs rather than meekly noting the
advice that is handed out, you will be much more likely to arrive
at an effective and economical plan of campaign.

With the aid of this book you can easily highlight the general
problem areas in your house and the most obvious solutions.

One complaint that readers sometimes have about a book like
this is that, for would-be burglars, it acts as a manual on how to
break into houses. In fact, of course, real burglars need no help
from us. But you, the householder, do need help in looking at
your house as a burglar would, so as to identify its weaknesses.

So the main part of this chapter unashamedly takes the form
of a burglary manual. It takes a student burglar on a tour of
your own house. It points out the good news and the bad news

that the student should be looking for. In the Checklist section at the end it tells *you*, the householder, where in this book you will find out how to turn the burglar's good news into bad — and how much that could cost.

The chapter assumes that you live, as many people do, in a semi-detached or detached house with front and back gardens. If you live in a terraced house or a flat, some things will not apply to you, and others will assume more significance.

Observation

As a student burglar, the first thing you have to learn is to look about you, and to make the most of what you see. The more you look, the more you will learn about your target and about the surrounding neighbourhood. Once you start breaking in you have little time, so find out all you can before you start.

Neighbours

Are there any neighbours around — more to the point, are there any *interested* neighbours? It is bad news if the neighbours obviously keep an eye on each other's property.

Appearances

Next, check whether the house looks occupied or not. Some things are a clear sign of an empty house: the daily growing stack of milk on the doorstep; the mail or newspapers choking the letter-box; the note pinned to the door. Some people like to leave everything tidy before they go on holiday, and make the place look unnaturally neat in the process — another sign that no one is at home.

Lighting

A house that is occupied in the evening will have lights shining, probably behind closed curtains, and probably being switched on and off in various rooms during the evening until, at bed-time, the lights retire upstairs. No lights at all is a pretty clear indication that no one is in. House lights which show no variation at all during the evening *may* simply have been left on by the householders when they left; but unless you're very keen it might be better to give that house a miss.

An outside light might be on, too. At night you want good cover: people may be more aware of the threat of burglary than they would be in the daytime, and your activities will look more suspicious. Outside lights may or may not mean that anyone is at home, but they certainly mean you will be more visible to anyone watching or passing.

Burglar alarms

If the house is fitted with a burglar alarm it will probably be obvious — a large alarm bell box under the eaves, visible from the road. Householders have been known to cheat, and use 'dummy' bell boxes; they have also been known to forget to switch the alarm on. And of course there may be ways into the house not protected by the alarm. But if the alarm is real, and switched on, and properly designed, you will find it very difficult to get into the house without setting it off. Unless you have a particular reason to burgle this particular house, you'd better move on.

Front door

Now walk confidently up to the front door, and ring the bell — just because you are a burglar there is no need to act like one. Take your time as you walk up the path, and you will learn a lot about the house — see 'The grounds and rear entrances', overleaf.

The front door is particularly interesting. On the one hand, you can be there legitimately: no one is going to give a second glance to someone reasonably dressed who is hanging around on a front doorstep. Another point in your favour is that the front door is usually what the experts call the *final exit door* — the one the occupiers leave by, which they can secure only from the outside with a key and not from the inside with additional bolts and so on. On the other hand, the front door is usually highly visible, and you cannot afford to waste much time doing anything suspicious.

As you wait, you can check the usual key-hiding places —

door mat, plant pot, dangling on a string just inside the letter-box, in the door itself. Note what sort of lock is fitted; if it is impressive, the whole house may be highly secure.

What's on offer?

If no one comes to the door, make the most of the opportunity to have a casual peer into the front windows to get an idea of what there is inside that's worth having. Look out for the tell-tale digital display of a video recorder, the gleam of polished silver candlesticks.

Foot in the door

If someone comes to the door, you will have to make a decision: should you try to force your way in, or tell the plausible story that you have prepared, and leave?

Front porch

A porch can be a help or a hindrance. It may be unlocked, or provided with very flimsy locks: once inside, you may be able to work away at the main house door unseen. But if the outer door is securely locked you may have to smash the porch glass before gaining even partial entry. And having to fight your way through two well-protected doors may just not be worth it.

The grounds and rear entrances

If you cannot easily enter through the front door, try the back. This might well be the next move of a legitimate caller who expected to find someone in, and allows you time to examine the grounds for potential and for snags. What you want, ideally, is plenty of cover to work in, but an easy exit in case you have to make a run for it. A high fence separating front and back gardens, with a locked gate, is bad news: it can make life very awkward and may rule out the back way in altogether.

Back door

At the back of the house you have a different set of pros and cons to consider. Assuming you are not overlooked by other houses, you have more time to work in, and more opportunity to attack the entry points violently without attracting attention. People are often far more casual about securing the backs of their homes, too. On the other hand, any neighbours who do see you are less likely to accept your presence without question, so you must still move quickly.

A back door is often bolted — bad news unless, as is likely, the bolts are not locked and there are glass panels you can break or a cat flap you can put your hand through. Even if the door is locked, it is surprising what a hefty kick with the heel of your boot can do.

Other doors

Traditional French windows are difficult to secure firmly, and are well worth investigating. They have small glass panels that you can break easily and quietly, and often poor locks and bolts that are easily opened. If you have time (as you often will have at the back of the house), you could attack the hinges, and open the doors along these edges.

Patio doors are difficult to secure — well worth trying to force, or even lever out of the way.

Windows

If you are having no luck with the doors, turn your attention to the windows — often the easiest way into a house, provided you can manage the acrobatics. Even occupiers who lock their doors securely may ignore the windows — possibly because there are so many designs of window that choosing suitable locks requires a good deal of research. From your point of view, the important point is that many windows are not even fastened.

Another great attraction of windows is that you can tell what problems they are going to present just by looking through them. If a window seems well secured, you may well think it not worth the bother of trying to open. On the other hand, if it is closed but not locked your next job is usually to smash the glass. This is relatively easy, especially if the panes are small, and with a bit of practice not very noisy either. The aim is not to climb through the broken pane, but to put your hand through it to undo the catches and open the window.

A sliding sash window is often attractive: original catches can often be undone simply by sliding a knife-blade along the crack between the two sashes. A louvre window may be even more straightforward: you might be able just to remove the blades of glass and reach in to open a catch. Leaded windows in an old property can often be dismantled pane by pane, with little more in the way of tools than a penknife; in a new house, you will know that the leading is merely a sham.

Double glazing is supposed (mainly by the people selling it) to be a great deterrent to burglars. But the double-glazing installation that impedes your progress significantly is exceptional. On the other hand, a closed venetian blind may well deter you, for some psychological reason.

Smart householders will have tried to catch you out by using some form of security glass on particularly vulnerable windows: it's worth knowing which types can easily be defeated.

Upstairs windows

Even people who routinely lock downstairs windows fail to lock all upstairs ones, so if you can climb up there easily you may find the house open to you. What about the drainpipes? Plastic ones are not easy to climb, but possible at a pinch, especially if you have to up go no further than the roof of a single-storey extension. Metal drainpipes are well worth trying — provided they have not been coated in anti-climb paint or some other slippery substance. Try also bathroom soil pipes: who puts locks on bathroom windows?

What about a ladder? They are often kept outside, because of their length, and are frequently not locked.

Outbuildings

If you are still having no joy with the house, what about sheds and garages? There is often nothing in them worth stealing, but there may well be tools which can be of assistance in breaking into the house.

Look at the doors and windows in the same way as you would for the house. There are likely to be many more points of weakness — broken and flimsy windows and doors; weak padlocks and bolts that can be levered away or even unscrewed; garage doors that can be forced open, or with locks that can easily be smashed off.

A quick look through the windows will tell you whether the stuff inside is going to be of any interest. Around Christmas and holiday times, you may not even need to break into the main house: the goods being stored in sheds and garages may be much more easily accessible, and very easily disposed of (drunk, eaten, or given away as presents).

Hidden entrance

Can you get into a garage attached to the house? Integral garages often have a door through to the house; once inside the garage, you can attack this door at leisure, probably using tools from the garage itself.

Once inside

You must make the best use of your limited time by going through as many drawers and belongings as you can. Don't try to be too clever and think of all the places where valuables may be hidden — just hope you pick on at least some of them.

Internal doors

Once you have broken in you may be faced with locked internal doors. These are not often a great worry, if you have a little time and are not worried about the noise. Try kicking them in, or picking the locks — they are usually simple.

Safe

If you find a safe, it may be worth trying to remove it from the house in its entirety — often quicker than trying to break into it on the spot.

Security marking

Before you take goods, check whether they are marked — owners often engrave a clever postcode-type mark on valuables. You may find such items difficult to dispose of, since they will more clearly be stolen.

Checklist

Outward signs

Neighbours Do you belong to a Neighbourhood Watch (page 31) or Good Neighbour Scheme (page 34)? *Cost* nothing, except an awareness of what is going on, and a commitment to take action when necessary.

Appearances Do you cancel services (milk, papers etc) before you go away — and in a way that does not draw attention to your holiday (page 26)? Will your neighbours help with deceiving appearances while you're away (page 29)?

Lighting Do you have adequate outside lighting, and do you keep it switched on at least all evening (page 27)? Do you leave lights burning inside the house when you are out — and do they make the place really look occupied (page 27)? *Cost* from £6 a year for the extra electricity, and £15 to £65 for automatic controls to switch lights on and off convincingly.

Burglar alarms

A burglar alarm (page 101) is expensive, and an imposition on your life. But it can stop a burglar before he even tries to break in. A dummy alarm (page 25) has some of the advantages of a real one, and costs much less. *Cost* about £150 for a do-it-yourself system; £700 for an extensive professionally installed one; £15 for a dummy bell box.

Front door

Locks can be a complicated subject, and one where it is easy to be blinded with science. Do you understand how locks work (page 44), the different features available, and what you should look out for when choosing a lock for a final exit door (page 58)? *Cost* £20 for a high-security lock of good quality.

What's on offer? Do you have valuables on display? Hiding them is an obvious and worthwhile precaution. *Cost* nothing except the inconvenience.

Foot in the door Is your front door fitted with a viewer (page 68) so you can check on your caller before opening the door? And does it have a strong door chain (page 66) to prevent him forcing his way in? *Cost* £4 each for a viewer and chain.

Front porch If you have an enclosed porch (page 96), have you fitted — *and* do you use — good locks on both doors? *Cost* £40 for both doors.

The grounds and rear entrances

Have you a high fence, with padlocked gate, separating front and rear gardens (page 97)? Check fences and hedges — can you reduce the cover behind which a thief could work, and yet still maintain good barriers?

Back door Are doors other than final exit doors protected with stout bolts (page 45), preferably lockable (page 48)? *Cost* £10 a door.

The strongest lock in the world is useless if the door it is fastened to is weak or rotten or a bad fit in its frame (page 42). Even a door in good condition may be inherently flimsy; some designs and materials are difficult to fit strong locks to, while others are simply too thin to fit good locks to (page 39). *Cost* £100 for a replacement door.

Other doors Provide the best fittings you can on French windows (page 60). *Cost* £40. Many patio doors need fitting with supplementary locks (page 61). *Cost* £10.

Windows

Make sure fixed windows really are unopenable. Fit window locks (page 79), make sure they are secure, and use them; but keep the key out of reach of anyone breaking the window. *Cost* £5 to £15 a window.

Sliding sash windows need special locks (page 83). *Cost* £4 for sliding sash window locks.

Leaded windows can be secured properly only by covering them with unbreakable glazing material (page 77). *Cost* from £40 a square metre.

Upstairs windows Fit locks to all windows that can be reached from single-storey roofs, balconies, bay windows, drainpipes and so on. If you must keep ladders outside, make sure they are well padlocked to special brackets or another secure fixing (even if you lock *all* upstairs windows, think of your neighbours). *Cost* £40 for a pair of brackets and padlocks.

Outbuildings

Make sure doors and windows on all outbuildings are in good condition (page 89). Fix padlocks securely to doors (page 90) and decide whether you need special fittings on garage doors (page 93). *Cost* £20 for a locking bar and padlock; £40 for special garage locks.

Consider covering up windows (page 90) and be especially careful over what you keep in your outbuildings (page 95).

Hidden entrance Treat a garage personal door as seriously as you would any outside door (page 95). *Cost* £30 for a high-security lock and bolts.

Once inside

Dividing up your valuables can make it less likely that a thief will have time to find them all (page 121). *Cost* a little inconvenience. Consider where you could store some items away from home, in a bank safe or similar (page 122). *Cost* £30 a year for storing jewellery you need a couple of times a year.

Internal doors There are pros and cons to locking internal doors (page 63). It may be worth doing on rooms that cannot be properly secured from outside attack. Fit a lock of reasonable quality so that it is not too easy to pick. *Cost* £12.

Safe An underfloor safe (page 127) mounted in a solid floor is likely to be the most secure type. *Cost* £200.

Security marking There is a postcode marking scheme (page 128), using engraving or invisible marking pens, that helps to make property less attractive to thieves and more likely to be recovered. *Cost* £2 for a marker pen, £10 for an engraving kit.

3
Making appearances deceptive

Burglars would make good social scientists. Their first job is to observe and evaluate — does this house look an easy target? If the answer is no, they are likely to move on to the next house.

False security

Almost without exception, your security devices should be real ones. If a thief gets close enough to see a lock or bolt, he is likely to try it anyway, just in case you might have left it open. So a dummy lock is not going to fool him.

But a dummy burglar alarm might: there is no way for an intruder to determine whether an alarm is real, and it would be risky to call your bluff. Dummy alarms are easy to fit; they consist of an empty alarm bell case (see page 101) that you mount high on the wall of your house where it will be visible from the road or an approach to the house. They are supplied by firms who make real alarms, and look just like the real thing – brightly painted, usually bearing a genuine alarm company's phone number and logo.

Even if you have a genuine alarm, a second dummy bell case mounted on a different wall of the house may be worthwhile.

Acting the part

The apparent presence of someone in your house is not guaranteed to deter burglars — especially those entering at dead of night. But an apparent absence of people is certainly a powerful attraction.

Look at houses. Notice for yourself how it is often easy to distinguish those that are occupied from those that are not. One of the problems in making your house look occupied when it is not is that the most obvious signs of occupancy are ones that you would not want to display in your absence — open doors and windows, for example. But there are other steps you can take.

Back in half an hour

However important it is to leave a message for someone you are expecting to call while you are out of the house, never leave notes pinned to the door: there is no way you can make these appear anything other than an invitation to a thief.

Holiday precautions

It's when you are on holiday that your house is going to look most unoccupied — when the serious burglar will have the opportunity to satisfy himself over a period of days that the coast is clear. Your neighbours can be of great help in making your house look occupied in a variety of ways, and keeping an eye open for callers. Their potential role is described in detail in the next chapter.

But you have your part to play, of course. Do not broadcast your future absence, in the pub or at the local shops, or even on your doorstep. For example, cancel newspapers by letter rather than in a visit to the newsagents (where you will have to announce your name, address and dates of absence to all in earshot). Cancel milk by letter, too — don't leave a note sticking out of a milk bottle.

Try not to advertise your departure too obviously — by spending half a day loading the car in the street, for example. And be careful not to give away your plans to strangers — however genuinely interested in your holiday they seem and however innocent their enquiries may sound.

Continue your deception, or rather your caution, even while you are away, by not giving your home address to anyone who does not need to know it. It is obviously imprudent to write it on luggage labels attached to the outside of your suitcases — but have you thought what a catalogue of empty homes is in every visitors' book you write in on your travels?

There are other precautions to be taken before you go away.

● Make doubly sure all your windows and doors are secure: follow the advice given in later chapters, and think about screwing shut any openings you are especially worried about (you may find you never need to open them again).

● Consider taking valuables to the bank (see page 122), which will certainly prevent their being stolen from home.

● Turn off the gas and water supplies.

● You will probably have to leave the electricity on to feed a freezer, a burglar alarm, or all your automatic lights (see below). But you may be able to remove some of the main fuses, to cut down the risk of faults causing fires. You should unplug all electrical equipment that is not going to be in use — but try to do so discreetly or it will advertise your absence to anyone who peers in.

Lighting

Many burglaries take place at night, when a thief can operate under cover of darkness and can check more easily than in daylight whether there is likely to be anyone at home. So lighting should be high on your list of deceiving devices — and modern electronics open up some sophisticated possibilities.

The first priority is simply to remember to keep some lights burning, whether you are at home or not — a house in darkness is a clear invitation to a thief to try his luck. But it is worth thinking about which lights will be effective in making the house look occupied.

A light in a hall only is not very convincing — on a par with hiding your door key under the front mat. One in a living room or kitchen is preferable during the evening — and it helps if the curtains or blinds are drawn, so that no one can see that the room is empty. External lighting is very important, making it much more difficult for a burglar to work unseen.

Automatic controls

Ordinary house lighting is fine if you are around now and then to switch it on and off — for example, switching it on at dusk before you go out for the evening, and altering its pattern at bedtime. It is not ideal if you have to leave a light burning all day because you won't be home until late that night. Automatic light switches can help; there are various kinds, which can produce quite different effects.

Timer Lights can be operated by a timer which switches them on and off at pre-set times each day. Versions are available which can be fitted in place of ordinary light switches, and provide normal on-off switching as well as timed switching. In one model, the exact moment of switching on and off varies randomly by a few minutes each day — this is supposed to deceive a thief who is 'staking out' your house and who would not be fooled by a precisely regular pattern of switching. For table lamps you can get timers which go between the plug and the existing wall socket.

Photo-cell From the deception point of view, a timer is a fairly blunt instrument, switching lights on and off irrespective of whether illumination is actually needed. A photo-cell reacts to the changing light conditions, and will switch a light on at dusk, and off again at dawn. This would hardly be appropriate for room lights, but can be useful for external lighting, giving light when it's needed but keeping down your electricity bills.

For lights inside the house, you can get a combined photo-cell and timer switch. This switches the light on when darkness falls and switches it off again at a pre-set time.

Proximity detector This device senses the presence of a person coming within its range of 'vision', and reacts by switching on a light. (It is very similar to the movement detectors described in Chapter 8.) You would normally position it on an outside wall, where it will sense people coming up to the house and switch on outside lights. This helps in several ways:
● the sudden illumination is a powerful deterrent to a thief, whose immediate reaction is to think that he has been spotted
● once on, the light will remain on for some time, even if the person steps outside the detector's field of view, reducing the chances of their being able to break into the house unseen
● it is one of the few security gadgets that not only provides a

warning to foes, but a positive welcome to friends, and to you if you return home after dark

● it can save electricity, and reduce the risk of annoying neighbours with outside lighting burning brightly all night.

You can get a proximity detector combined with one or two lights, but a separate unit that will switch a number of lights has advantages — you can place such a detector where it will 'watch' the most likely approach to the house, and place the lights where they will do most good in illuminating entry points to the house itself. Some care is necessary in setting up the detector so that it does not react without good reason — to animals, for example, or passers-by in the street. (In country areas, lights going on and off all night in response to passing animals may do more harm than good, making you think the house is being approached by intruders when it's not.)

If you want to control very powerful lights, check that the device will switch the wattage you have in mind.

Curtains Automatic lighting controls are all very well, but the problem of curtains remains. Turning lights on in rooms which have the curtains left open may not persuade a thief that you are at home. On the other hand, leaving curtains closed all day is a clear advertisement that the house is unoccupied.

One solution is a helpful neighbour, to close and open curtains for you; they could also switch the lights on and off, but if you leave this bit of the job to automatic controls you are more likely to be able to complete the illusion of occupancy by switching lights off at bedtime. Another possibility is to use roller or venetian blinds: it is quite usual to find them closed during the day, so leaving them closed need not give the game away. Or think about lighting rooms that cannot themselves be seen into, but with doorways that will let light into other, more accessible rooms.

If you have to choose, it's certainly better to have lights burning in rooms with curtains open in the evening than to have curtains closed all day.

4
Friends and neighbours

Among your most valuable weapons for fighting burglary are people. A thief is much less likely to work on a house that is — or more to the point might be — occupied or overlooked. Give him sufficient evidence that his activities are likely to be detected and he will go away.

When you are away from home, other people, especially your near neighbours, can help to conceal the fact. And they can be your eyes and ears to check on suspicious happenings. In turn, of course, you can do the same for them.

Although an informal 'please keep your eye on things while I'm away' approach is better than nothing, people can be of more help to each other if they know in more detail what they are supposed to be doing, and feel they have the authority to act on each other's behalf. There are two types of scheme for arrangements: the **Neighbourhood Watch** scheme, which covers a large area, from a street to an entire housing estate; and the **Good Neighbour Scheme**, which is an arrangement between you and your close neighbours for when you are on holiday.

Neighbourhood Watch

The main point of a Neighbourhood Watch scheme is simply to raise people's awareness of burglary — of how it could happen to their own houses; of what innocent-looking activities might be a prelude to a break-in; and of what to do if anything suspicious does happen.

Starting a scheme is simple. The first step is to get in touch with your local police station and arrange to discuss the matter with your area's Crime Prevention Officer (CPO) or your local 'beat' officer. He or she will know whether there are other schemes operating in the area, and will explain how you would go about organizing yours. It is usually a matter of:

● deciding what area any scheme should cover

● finding out whether sufficient people in that area are interested in co-operating (the police may circulate letters and leaflets)

● arranging a public meeting at which the police will outline the scheme (if there is enough interest)

● appointing co-ordinators to manage the scheme when it is in operation; these should be people who normally spend a lot of time at home, especially during the day, so that they will be more likely to be available if they are needed

● letting everyone know — residents and would-be burglars — when the scheme is under way. There are stickers you can put on your doors and windows, and you may get permission from your local council to have 'Neighbourhood Watch' signs attached to lamp posts.

How you watch

Some people are put off the idea of a Neighbourhood Watch scheme because it smacks of snoopers prying into other people's business and vigilantes taking the law into their own hands. There may be some justification for this idea in America, where there are often active patrols by the local people — but this is neither encouraged nor common in Britain.

In the UK, the scheme is more passive, and the only requirement for participants is that they should not shut their eyes to goings-on around them. You are not expected to take shifts in watching the area, or even to alter your daily routine, but simply to report to one of the co-ordinators anything that you do notice as you go about your normal activities. They will pass details on to the police. Of course, if you were to notice anything that clearly needed immediate attention, you would dial 999 and report it directly to the police — and being part of a Neighbourhood Watch scheme may make you feel less inhibited about this.

Making you more aware

The scheme also acts as a focus for promoting more general crime prevention matters in the area. Participants may be encouraged to arrange individual visits from CPOs to check the security of their own houses. It can make you more likely to go to the police with other problems. There are also theories that it improves relationships between the police and the local community; and that it reduces the fear of crime by showing you what can be done to reduce it. One group reported that their scheme had important social spin-offs: neighbours got to know each other and arranged social events that would not have happened otherwise.

Does it work?

There is conflicting evidence about the overall success of Neighbourhood Watch schemes — though the schemes have not been going long enough for many formal studies of them to have been carried out.

Results available in early 1987 from the best schemes quote remarkable reductions in crime: 78 per cent down in a scheme in Washington New Town, for example. And there is a lot of enthusiasm for setting up schemes — now totalling over 30,000. On the other hand, one two-year study of two supposedly 'good' schemes showed no decrease in crime at all. And there is some evidence that they may not *reduce* crime so much as *move* it — either to a next-door area that doesn't have a scheme, or to other categories of crime: street muggings, say.

The problem with this sort of displacement of crime is that it can push it into areas where it is more difficult to deal with: shopping areas; inner-city districts and so on. It is much harder to get successful Watch schemes going in such areas, where they are needed most, than in areas where crime is less of a problem, and where relationships between the police and the community are already good. So it may be short-sighted to look simply at the drop in crime figures in areas with Neighbourhood Watch schemes if, over the country as a whole, they are making life harder for police. But generally the police encourage the formation of such schemes.

Some insurance policies offer reduced premiums to house-holders whose security precautions meet certain standards and who are members of a Neighbourhood Watch scheme.

Good Neighbour Scheme

This scheme is much more specific than Neighbourhood Watch, though it shares one of the same ideas of allowing neighbours to take responsibility for acting in your absence — in this case, absence for a long period such as a holiday.

You fill in a card giving your holiday address, dates when you will be away, where and how you can be contacted in emergencies, and so on. You give this to a neighbour who has agreed to look after your home, and fill in a similar card to hand in at your police station; this card includes details of your neighbour, so that everyone is clear who is in charge.

When you're away

It is up to you and your neighbour to agree how your house should be looked after. There are a number of possibilities.

• They should at least check your letter-box every day, and remove letters and papers from where they can be seen. Anything sticking out of a letter-box is an obvious give-away, and mail lying on the floor can often be seen through a glass door. But don't forget that even with a solid door someone could look through the letter-box.

• They can make your house look occupied without going inside — by putting out washing in the garden, perhaps, or parking a car in your drive from time to time.

• If you are away for a long time, they might keep the garden from looking too overgrown. Invite them to pick fruit and vegetables: they will be over-ripe and no use to you when you return, and again it will make the place look more naturally occupied.

• They can keep an eye open for callers. Some may well be on legitimate business, and can be dealt with or put off until your return (but even these should not be told that you are away for a period). Others will get the clear message that your place is under watch.

● In the evening, they could close your curtains and switch on some lights, returning before bedtime to switch off the lights, and again first thing the next morning to open the curtains.

● They could water any house-plants. Though there are other ways of keeping them alive while you are away, it makes the place much more lived-in if all your plants are in their usual places, and looking alive and well.

Whatever your neighbours do, you should expect to return the favour when they go away.

House-sitting

The ultimate way of compensating for your absence from home is to have your home actually occupied while you are away. This is especially helpful if you have pets, and will probably be better for them than putting them into kennels or catteries. A friend or neighbour, particularly if they live alone, may welcome the opportunity to house-sit for you. A house-swapping holiday is another way of keeping your house occupied — though you would probably not want to embark on such a holiday solely for that reason. There are also commercial firms who run live-in caretaking services for a fee: of course, you will want to satisfy yourself that their house-sitters are completely trustworthy.

If you do get someone else to occupy your home while you're away, bear in mind that they must be familiarised not only with your security arrangements but also with your fire safety arrangements (see Chapter 10).

5
Doors and door locks

However casual you are about the prospect of burglary, you are almost certain to have at least some form of rudimentary security on your main house doors. But the key word is 'rudimentary': far too many homes are equipped with door locks which present only trivial obstacles to a determined and experienced burglar: the back door fitted with only a two-lever mortice lock, say, and the front door protected by a non-dead-locking cylinder rim latch.

By the end of this chapter, you will know exactly what these unfamiliar technical terms mean, and why locks such as these are virtually an invitation to competent thieves to walk in and help themselves.

But before you can decide on the types of lock you need to protect your house, you must first study your doors and their surrounding frames — how they are constructed and what condition they are in. It is a waste of time and money to fit good locks if they are not suited to the type of door, or if the doors or their frames are themselves in need of repair or even complete replacement.

If you are buying a new door, do think seriously about getting a new frame to go with it: you will need to anyway if the new door is thicker than the old one. Remember also that door frames rely for much of their strength on their fixing; if possible, they should be built into the adjacent walls.

In the main, this chapter is about outside doors — ones that lead to your garden, or the street, or perhaps to an unprotected glazed porch or conservatory. The question of locking inside doors is another matter; see page 63.

Types of door

There is more to door construction than meets the eye and, in considering the security of your doors and how to improve it, the first stage is to work out what forms of construction your doors use. There are four main forms.

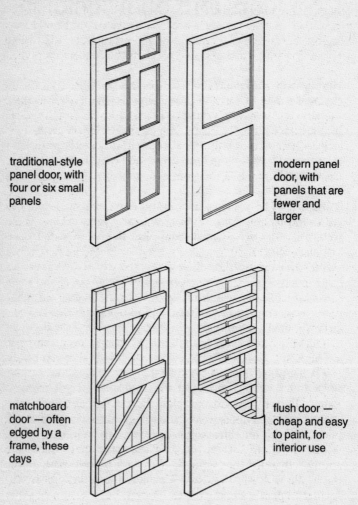

traditional-style panel door, with four or six small panels

modern panel door, with panels that are fewer and larger

matchboard door — often edged by a frame, these days

flush door — cheap and easy to paint, for interior use

Panel doors

Most external doors are *panel doors*. These are made of a framework of thickish timbers forming the top, bottom and sides, usually with at least one more horizontal cross-piece. (Horizontal pieces are usually called *rails*; the vertical ones *stiles*.) The holes in the framework are filled in with wood or glass panels. These doors, if well constructed, can be relatively strong; but there are several things to look out for, either when appraising your existing doors, or when choosing a new door.

Frame The framework will usually be stronger if made of hardwood than of softwood. Unless you are an expert in these matters, you will find it difficult to tell much about the type of wood of an existing door. But if you are buying a new door, it is usually possible to find out the type of wood used in it — Brazilian, Red Meranti or Lauan hardwoods, Redwood or Canadian Hemlock softwoods are often used these days.

Thickness The thicker a door is, the better the security it can offer. Most doors these days are about 44mm (1¾in) thick; some cheaper doors are 40mm, which is really bordering on being too thin. A 50mm (2in) thick door would be better, but you might have difficulty finding one.

As important as thickness is the width of the stiles, and again the wider the better (the ultimate being a solid door made entirely of framework, with no thin panels to weaken the structure at all — but these are rare).

Thickness and stile width both affect not only the basic strength of the door, but also the types of lock that you can fit (see 'Choosing a lock', page 58).

Panels Before plywood and other sheet materials were invented, the panels in doors were made of thin planks of solid wood, normally with an extra vertical piece of framework running down the centre of the door. These traditional doors are stronger than the modern-style ones with larger panels across the whole width of the door. Whatever the style of door, the smaller its panels are, the better — partly because it means that the framework of the door is thicker and stronger, partly because it makes it more difficult for a thief to kick them in.

A wood panel is usually stronger than a glass one of the same size. But if you have the choice, it would be better to go for a thicker, stronger door with glass panels than a thin door with wood panels — particularly as in a thin door the wood panels themselves are likely to be also thin and perhaps not well secured to the framework. Though glass panels may seem very vulnerable, there are types of glass which are less easy to smash than plywood. See page 76 for details.

Matchboard doors

These simply constructed doors were once standard equipment for country cottages and are often used to give a rustic look to a house. They consist of vertical tongue-and-groove boards forming a large panel nailed to large horizontal rails (*ledges*) on the back surface. Original examples can be very massive indeed, consisting of thick, wide boards — but their apparent security is often spoiled by a weak fixing to the frame.

Modern equivalents are formed more like a traditional panel door, with framework around at least the sides and top, and ledges across the middle and bottom. Often there are diagonal framework pieces too (*braces*), mainly to stop the door sagging into a diamond shape, but also helping security. The whole construction forms a 'framed, ledged, and braced matchboard door'. But the material is normally softwood, the framework is often relatively narrow, and the matchboarding may not be securely attached to it. All in all, these are probably not as strong as most panel doors.

Flush doors

These have the appearance of solid wood doors, with flat, smooth surfaces on each face; but they are in fact relatively flimsy. They have a relatively narrow framework, which is usually supplemented by larger blocks of wood at the points where locks and hinges will be fitted. Over this on both sides are fastened wood sheets, usually plywood or hardboard. The void between the two sheet sides is filled in one of several ways — with a sort of cardboard honeycomb, for example.

Flush doors are often used for inside doors, and can be very cheap. These can certainly not be used for outside doors: they wouldn't stand up to the weather and they would be a very poor security risk. It is possible to get flush doors meant for external use, but they are mostly not as strong as a panelled door.

French windows

French windows are invariably a weak point. They are fully glazed, which makes them vulnerable unless security glass is used. And they traditionally come in pairs; the meeting point between the two doors is weak because each is relying on the other to act as its frame, which is something a door is not very good at. They are often also outward-opening, which means that the hinges are exposed to attack (see page 48).

Patio doors

Patio doors — sliding doors consisting largely of glass — bring several problems. First, the fact that they are sliding doors means that they require special locks. They almost always have an aluminium framework, and an aluminum surrounding frame, which is difficult (though not impossible, see page 61) to fit additional locks to — a problem only because many patio doors have inadequate locks in the first place. Often, a thief can overcome the original locks simply by levering the door off its bottom track using a garden spade.

The fact that they are large, and largely glass, is paradoxically a help rather than a hindrance. They are invariably fitted with toughened glass for safety reasons, and usually with double glazing — so smashing the glass is difficult and may be practically impossible. In any case, burglars don't like breaking large panes: it makes too much noise.

Aluminium doors

Though most hinged doors are wood, aluminium-framed ones are also available, and are often fitted in a house at the same time as aluminium windows are installed to replace wooden ones.

Like patio doors, they suffer from the problem that additional locks cannot easily be fitted, and that the ones supplied with the door may not be particularly secure. If you are having a replacement door fitted, make sure it comes with a lock made to the British Standard (see page 62).

Security doors

Special security doors are available. These usually incorporate a layer of steel sheet, and come as a unit complete with surrounding frame and special locks. The cost of such doors could be justified only if your home is secure in every other way.

Door handing

When specifying some locks, it's important to know how the door opens — its *handing*. There are four possible variations as viewed from outside the house (or from a particular room, for inside doors): the door will open either inwards or outwards, and will have the lock on either the left or the right.

Door and frame faults

Whatever type of door you have, it is no good unless it is securely hung in its frame (which is in turn securely fastened to the wall) and fits the frame snugly all round. Gaps between the door and frame make it easier for a burglar to insert a lever to force the door open.

Fitting If there are gaps between a door and its frame — probably because the door has shrunk — consider fixing strips of wood to the door or frame to fill them. On the other hand, tightness — preventing the door from closing fully at all points around the edge — may be caused simply by a build-up of paint on the door or frame, or perhaps improperly fitted draught-excluding material. Correct such faults before thinking of planing the edge of the door.

Warping A warped door can often be corrected by forcing it to twist in the opposite direction and holding it in that position for several days, with wedges and nails. But that is unlikely to be possible with an external door. If the warp is slight you may be able to alter the frame to fit the door, rather than vice-versa, either by trimming pieces out of the *stop* — the piece of the frame which sticks out to meet the face of the door when it is closed — or by adding bits on.

Many stops are not an integral part of the frame, but are separate pieces of wood nailed on; a *planted* stop like this can be removed and fixed in a new position to match the door's warp.

Hinges Check that the hinges are properly screwed to the door and frame; if the screws are loose, remove and replace them either with longer ones or (if the holes in the hinge will take it) with fatter ones. External doors really need three hinges — top, bottom and middle — rather than just two. The door should close easily; any resistance or evident strain on the hinges is usually a sign that the door has been incorrectly fitted in the first place — perhaps the recesses for the hinges have been cut too deeply. Or, again, it may be a problem with paint or draught excluders on the hinge side of the door or frame that needs correcting.

Loose joints You should not be able to make the door move at the joints by twisting it or lifting it at the lock side. Loose joints mean the door will be easier to kick in. It is possible to strengthen a door simply by screwing large metal plates across the joints. There are other methods which are more aesthetic-ally pleasing, but require more carpentry skill: with traditional mortise-and-tenon joints, for example, by re-wedging the tenons; or inserting dowel pegs into them through the face of the stiles; or dismantling the door altogether and re-assembling with modern glues.

Damage Previous attempts to force a door (or just years of door-slamming) may have weakened or split the wood around the site of the door lock, and the *staple* on the frame. Treat these weaknesses particularly seriously, and either reinforce the woodwork at these places, preferably with pieces of steel, or replace the door or frame. If you are fitting a new frame, or judge that the existing one is in need of securing in place, do not skimp on the fixings – use the fattest and longest screws you can manage (using a brace and bit to drive them if necessary).

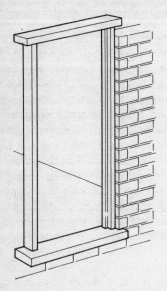

door frame without door —
showing how the frame is built into
the brickwork

Bolts and locks explained

Although it may seem that the dozens of locks on the market all
have their own highly technical characteristics there are in fact
only a few basic lock features — the confusion lies in the possible
permutations of these features.

It is important to understand these basic features before you
go on to decide which type of lock best suits each door in your
house. So this section looks at locks from the basic principles
upwards, through the two main lock types, then on to ways in
which lock security can be increased, and finally on to the
added features which do more to increase convenience in fitting
and use than to enhance security.

Various words in the following descriptions are picked out in
bold type; these are names you'll come across in manufacturers'
literature and advertisements — though you will also encounter
variations on these themes.

The basic theory

The only practical way to temporarily prevent a door from opening is to place a bar across both it and the frame, and secure it to both the door and the frame so that the door cannot be swung open. Almost always, the bar takes the form of a **bolt** which is slid across the door into a hole in the frame, or a metal socket on it, called a **staple**. With an ordinary bolt, that is all you get — and although bolts are very useful, anyone can operate them, including thieves. Some sort of bolt can give adequate security for many doors which are secured from inside the house. But there is always at least one door which you must secure as you leave, from outside — the **final exit door**. Any such door must have a **lock**. This still employs a bolt, but it can be operated only by a **key** which can be removed from the lock so that unauthorized people cannot use it. Locks are often used on doors which are not final exit doors, and must be used on such doors where an intruder could gain access to a simple bolt — by breaking a glass pane, for example.

Bolts and bolt locks

House doors other than final exit doors can be secured from inside the house, which simplifies matters considerably. The main kinds of bolt you might use are listed below; there are others covered in other chapters, eg for sheds and garages.

Tower and barrel bolts These are common-or-garden surface-mounted bolts, as sold by every ironmonger: a rounded bar running through a guide screwed to the door and shooting into a staple screwed to the door frame (or, sometimes, into a hole in the frame itself). Barrel bolts have a full-length guide; tower bolts have two or more short guides with gaps in between.

Fit the largest bolts you can bear the sight of; small ones are not very secure. This is not so much because the bar is likely to give under attack, but because almost all the security rests on the screws that hold the guide and staple in place, and a small bolt allows you to use only small screws (and not many of them). Large screws will give more security — if you fix them firmly.

These bolts are not lockable, so they depend for their security on being inaccessible even to a violently disposed intruder; do not use them on glazed or thin-panelled wood doors.

tower bolt, with short guides

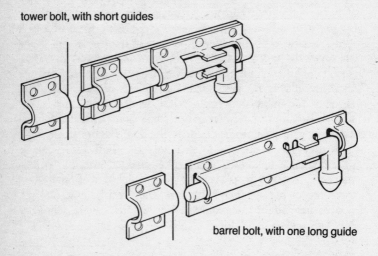

barrel bolt, with one long guide

Flush bolts These work in the same way as barrel bolts, but are recessed into the door surface. You could use one where you want a neater appearance than a barrel or tower bolt gives. But their main use is to secure one leaf of a double door.

Mortice bolts These are mounted within the woodwork of the door, and shoot into the woodwork of the surrounding frame, so they look neater than a simple barrel or tower bolt; they can be smaller, too, since their security depends on the strength of the door and frame rather than relying on screws. You operate most types with a simple key having raised teeth along a straight shaft; these mate with a toothed 'rack' on the bolt and as you turn the key it shoots the bolt in or out. But variants are now appearing which are operated by more complex keys.

Mortice bolts are fairly easy to fit; the job consists mainly of drilling a mortice in the edge of the door to take the body of the device, another hole from the inside of the door to take the key, and a third in the surrounding frame to act as the staple.

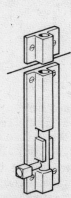

smaller barrel bolts, with a brass
finish, are often to be seen on
French windows, where
appearance is important

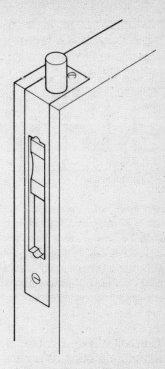

a better solution is flush bolts, set
into the edge of the door

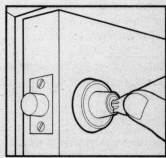

mortice bolts, with simple and more elaborate key (ERA)

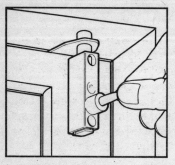 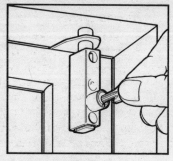

lockable bolts, with simple and more elaborate key (ERA)

Lockable bolts These are surface-mounted barrel-type bolts with a simple lock mechanism, usually offering a reasonable range of key differs (see opposite), which makes them an advance in that respect on mortice rack bolts. But small ones, using small screws for fixing, will not be very secure. One type has the considerable advantage that it locks automatically as you slide it shut; you need a key only to open it again.

Dog (hinge) bolts These bolts are mounted on the hinge side of the door, recessed into the door edge but permanently protruding from it. One edge is chamfered so that it moves easily in and out of its staple as the door is opened or closed.

Their main use is on doors that open outwards, where the hinges are exposed to attack: a thief could knock out the hinge pin (which holds the two leaves of a hinge together), for example, and lever the door open.

dog bolt, to make the hinge side of the door secure (ERA)

Lock mechanisms

All mechanical locks work on much the same principle. Inside the lock are pieces of metal which can be moved by the key — either as you push the business end of your key (the **bit**) into the lock, or as you start to turn it. If the shape of the bit is correct it will move the metal pieces into the one correct position which allows the bolt to move as you turn the key. If the bit is the wrong shape, the internal metal pieces will move to the wrong position, the key won't turn and the bolt won't move.

The main types of lock

There are only two main types of mechanism arising from the basic principles explained above — the **lever lock** and the **cylinder lock**. Each type allows a number of different locks to be made, each with a matching key which won't open the others; each different one is called a **differ**. Other things being equal, the more differs a particular design of lock has, the better — the less likely it is that someone else's key will fit your lock.

The section which follows explains how the two types of lock work. If this doesn't interest you, skip to 'More about lock bolts', page 52.

In a **lever lock** the metal pieces are large plates, pivoted at one end and with a slot (**gate**) cut into each one. Only when these slots are aligned together can the **bolt stump** (a bar attached to the bolt) slide through them, so that the bolt itself can move in or out. When the lock has no key in it, the slots are not aligned, but as you turn the key the notches cut in its bit mean that the levers are lifted to different degrees — so the gates line up, and the bolt can move. The key cleverly provides the motive force needed to move the bolt as you turn it.

In a **cylinder lock** the mechanism is separate from the bolt itself, and consists of a fixed outer metal cylinder with a snugly-fitting inner core (**plug**) which the key slides into and which is connected to the lock bolt; when the plug turns, the bolt shoots in or out. Almost all cylinder locks are of the **pin-tumbler** type. Drilled into the wall of the cylinder are a series of shafts, each containing a spring and a metal rod (**driver**); in the 'resting' position each driver is pushed into a

pin-tumbler cylinder, without key

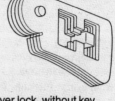

lever lock, without key

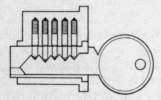

pin-tumbler cylinder, with key in place and all the pins lined up, allowing the cylinder to turn

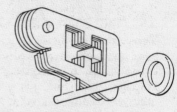

lever lock, with key half-turned and all the gates lined up, allowing the bolt stump to move

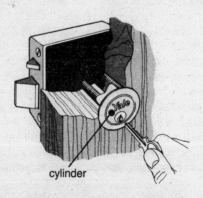

cylinder

a typical installation of a cylinder rim lock, showing how the cylinder into which the key slots is physically separate from the main body of the lock containing the bolt (Yale)

corresponding shaft in the plug which contains another rod (called a **pin**) the length of which varies from one shaft to the next. The driver acts as a bolt in its own right, locking the plug to the cylinder and preventing it from being turned. As you insert a key, the serration on its bit pushes the pins up by differing amounts, and so the driver, against the spring; if it's the right key, the driver is pushed just home into the cylinder, and the pin stays just in the plug: then the plug is free to turn, and so to operate the lock bolt.

Increasing security

A key 'fits' a lock only if its bit is shaped so that it aligns correctly *all* the levers or pins in the lock. You could make a lock with only one lever or one pin; but such a design would permit only a small number of key differs (so other people's keys would be quite likely to fit) and would be very easily 'picked' — a thief could improvise a 'key' to open the lock by trial and error. The more levers or pins, the greater the number of possible differs — a lock used on a final exit door should normally have at least five, which (depending on other aspects of a lock's design) allows many thousands of differs.

There is one more device that helps to increase a lock's security — a **ward**. This is a series of metal pieces set around the inside of the lock's keyhole that prevent the key from turning unless its bit is shaped with sections cut away (also called wards) in the appropriate places to avoid the obstructions. It is more of an added irritation to a lock-picker than a genuine increase in security: if you make a key with sufficient amounts of the bit cut away (which is what a **skeleton key** is) then it will pass over a range of differently-positioned wards. On the other hand, there are so many possible arrangements of wards that it would be impossible to cut a single skeleton key that would pass over all of them.

Keys for pin-tumbler cylinder locks have a slightly different system of 'wards': the sides of the slot you push the key into before you turn it are usually given a zig-zag shape, and the key sides must have a corresponding zig-zag profile — otherwise you won't be able to push the key into the slot at all, never mind turn it to open the lock.

More about lock bolts

The type of bolt described so far is a simple bar of metal which cannot be moved, either to open or close the lock, without the key. This type of bolt — called a **deadbolt** — is certainly very secure, but a lock which offers no other way of holding the door closed — a **deadlock** — would be highly inconvenient: everyone passing through the door would have to unlock it and then lock it again, using a key. So most doors also have another kind of bolt to hold the door closed rather than to lock it — a **springbolt** or **latch** — operated only by a knob or handle which is fixed to the door. The bolt is spring-loaded so that it normally remains shot out of the lock, and the face that hits the door frame first is sloped or rounded so that it is forced in against the spring if you push the door closed without turning the knob.

A lock with both a deadbolt and a separate springbolt is a **sashlock**, which provides both security and convenience in a single lock. Many people who want that combination rely on a **nightlatch**, which has a springbolt operated by a knob on the inside of the door but a key on the outside; but this is far from ideal. The main problem is with glazed doors, or ones with thin wood panels: a thief could simply smash the panel and open the door by twisting the inside lever. Or he might be able to slide a flexible strip into the gap between the door and the frame, and push the springbolt back into the lock (though, unless your door is a very poor fit in its frame, this isn't the nonchalantly easy business with a credit card that TV films would have you believe).

The solution to these problems is to fit a **deadlockable springbolt** lock. This too is operated by a key from outside the door, and a knob from the inside; but the springbolt is (or can be) transformed into a deadbolt when the door is closed — so that it cannot be pushed back against the spring. With some, after slamming the door shut you throw the bolt further into the staple by a turn of the key from the outside, in the same way as you would lock a normal deadbolt. Others are **automatically deadlocking** as you shut them. But this still leaves the possibility that a thief who gains access to the knob on the inside will be able to open the lock. The solution is to make the knob lockable too: sometimes this is done as you deadlock the door from outside; with other models the handle is locked with the key from inside, before you leave the house.

The two types of fixing

There remains one main way in which locks vary: how they are fixed to the door. There are two main types — **mortice** and **rim** locks. Either type may be fitted with either cylinder or lever locking mechanisms — but in practice most mortice locks use a lever mechanism, and probably all good-security rim locks use a cylinder mechanism.

Mortice locks

These are fitted into a slot (or mortice) cut into the door edge. This looks neat — you can hardly see the lock at all, even when the door is open — and it is impossible to prize the lock off the door when it is locked. On the other hand, cutting a slot in the door edge inevitably weakens it, and makes the door easier to kick in. A mortice lock would certainly be a poor choice for a door less than 44mm thick (though many locks claim to be suitable for doors down to about 38mm thick).

As well as thickness, you need also to consider the *width* of your door stile. **Lock cases** (the boxes that hold the lock mechanism and have to be accommodated in the mortice) are commonly either about 75mm deep (3in) or 64mm (2½in) — often called a **narrow-stile** version. But what stile width will be needed in practice varies from lock to lock — in some cases, a manufacturer will claim that the stile needs to be only a millimetre or so wider than the quoted case depth; in others they may require the stile to be at least 5mm wider than the case depth. So don't go just by the lock's nominal size — check before buying that it is actually suitable.

Cutting the slot in a new door to take a mortice lock needs some carpentry skill: it must be a tight fit, to ensure that the lock receives maximum support from the door, and that the door is weakened as little as possible. And to make sure the door closes easily, the lock must be absolutely square-on to the door edge in all three directions.

Replacing an existing lock may be easier: many lock cases are of a standard size, with standard positions for keyholes and door knob shafts. So you may have to do no more than prize out the existing lock (though this is not always a trivial task) and push home the new one. One dimension often quoted to help you match a new lock to an old one is the **backset** — the distance from the edge of the door to the centre of the keyhole. But if you want to be absolutely certain a new lock will directly replace an old one, you would need to remove the old one first and take it to the shop.

There is little point in fitting a new lock if the old one is a loose fit in its mortice, or if the part of the door around the lock has been weakened (perhaps in a burglary attempt). Either replace the door, or fit the new lock in a different position, filling in the old mortice with hardwood pieces cut to a tight fit and glued in place.

Weakened or split timber will have to be cut out entirely and replaced, or strengthened (on both sides of the door) with steel plates: you may be able to set these into recesses chiselled out of the face of the door but, for strength if not for looks, it would be better simply to mount them on the surface. (Don't use normal screws to fix the outside plate — see page 91 for more secure alternatives.)

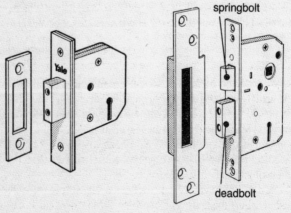

mortice lever deadlock (Yale)   mortice lever sashlock (Yale)

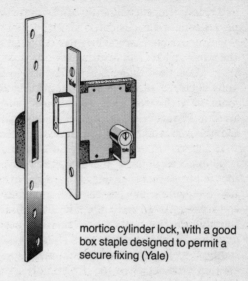

mortice cylinder lock, with a good
box staple designed to permit a
secure fixing (Yale)

The staple is also recessed, into the door frame. In its
simplest form the staple need be no more than a small slot cut
into the frame, but this is far from ideal. At the very least there
should be a **striking plate** fitted over the slot to protect the door
frame from wear and tear. Many striking plates include a **box
staple** which further protects the frame and makes it more
difficult for a burglar to cut out the frame and gain access to the
lock bolt.

Rim locks

These are screwed to the surface on the inside of the door. A rim
lock is much easier to fit than a mortice lock, and does not
weaken the door — so it is a better choice for thinner doors. But
it depends for its security on how well it is screwed to the door.
This goes for the staple as well, which also has to be surface-
mounted on the frame — and because it is smaller than the lock
it is even more difficult to fix securely.

The screws holding a rim lock and its staple in place are
concealed when the door is closed, so that a thief cannot simply
unscrew the lock after having smashed a glass or wooden panel

in the door. But there is always the risk that a rim lock could be prized away from the door.

Rim locks are more tolerant of door thickness than mortice ones: most will suit doors between 38mm and 60mm thick, and some will cope with even thinner doors (though such doors are unlikely to be secure enough in themselves) or thicker ones (unusual in houses). But many demand quite wide stiles: around 90mm is quite usual, though narrow-stile versions about 64mm long are also available.

Fitting a rim lock involves nothing more than drilling a large-diameter hole in the stile, and maybe chiselling out a couple of recesses (like ones for hinges) in the door and frame edges. Again, a replacement lock might fit the existing holes and recesses; and in any case it is not so disastrous if these need slightly enlarging or shifting in position, because the amount of extra wood you remove is unlikely to weaken the door significantly. But, as for a mortice lock, make sure you attend to any existing weaknesses in the door before fitting a new lock. In particular, be wary of re-using existing screw holes as they stand: you may not be able to make the new fixing as secure as the original. If you cannot use longer or fatter screws than originally fitted, fill in the holes with tight-fitting plugs of wood glued into place, and start from scratch.

Take particular care in fitting the staple. Some staples have extra-long front plates which help to ensure a firm fixing.

lever rim lock — not so common
these days, but still available

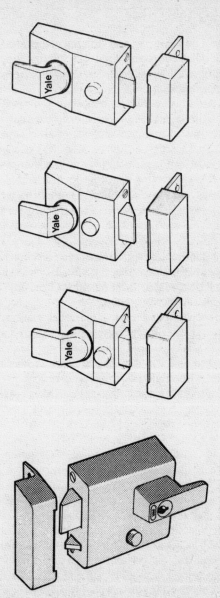

simple cylinder
rim locks in
different lengths
to suit different
widths of door
stile (Yale)

more complex
cylinder rim
lock, with
automatic
deadlocking
and a lockable
internal knob
(Yale)

Choosing a lock

Armed with all the knowledge of the last few pages on lock technology, you can now go on to choose locks suitable for each of your external doors. Some suggestions for particular types and situations of door follow.

In overall terms there is nothing to choose in performance between the main styles of lock – rim or mortice; cylinder or lever. There are secure and insecure versions of all types: see page 62 for advice on choosing a secure version. Mortice locks tend to be cheaper than rim locks offering the same degree of security, though the cost of having a mortice lock fitted for you by a professional (especially into a new door) might outweigh this difference.

Final exit door

The most important door to deal with first is what is called your *final exit door* since, as explained on page 45, this one can be protected only by a lock operated from outside. These pointers may help you to narrow down your choice.

● What about the door's **construction** — is it thick enough for a mortice lock? Are the stiles too narrow for a standard-width case?

● If the door is **glazed** and you choose a springbolt lock you *must* be able to lock the internal knob.

● If you want to fit a **replacement** lock easily it makes sense to stick to the original type.

● On a **new door**, a rim lock would be easier to fit than a mortice one.

● The type most **convenient in use** is probably an automatic deadlocking springbolt: just slam the door behind you as you rush down the road for the bus.

The ideal is to fit *two* locks — one about a third of the way up from the bottom, the other a third of the way down from the top (you will not be able to do this on a flush door unless you know it has suitably placed lock blocks). One can be an automatic deadlocking springbolt (almost certainly a cylinder rim lock); the other a simple deadbolt (probably a mortice lock, either lever or cylinder). This combination probably allows the best compromise between maximum security when you are out (provided you discipline yourself always to lock the deadbolt) and easy exit in case of fire — if you leave the deadbolt unlocked when you are in the house (see Chapter 10).

Other main outside doors

Outside doors that are not final exit doors are in one sense easier to deal with, because you have a range of devices other than locks that you can fit — see 'Bolts and bolt locks', page 45. On the other hand, they can be more difficult because they are often 'problem' doors, such as the French windows or patio doors discussed below, and are often in secluded positions favoured by burglars.

They are probably doors that you pop in and out of quite often, so you will need a non-locking latch to hold the door closed but still openable from either side without a key. To make the door secure, you can of course add a deadlock of some sort, but there may be no need. For a sturdy wood-panelled door, simple bolts top and bottom would be sufficient. On a glazed door, or one with large thin wood panels, these would need to be lockable.

Garage personal door

Houses with integral garages often have a 'personal' door between the house and garage. Though the garage itself should be locked (see Chapter 7), the personal door ought to be locked too, as a second line of defence.

The door is likely to be a flush type, but it should be of fairly heavy construction to meet fire safety regulations. So you should be able to fit a mortice lock without weakening it — and a rim lock on a flush door often looks out of place.

A garage personal door may be subject to a violent attack — if a thief has got that far he probably has access to some useful tools, and can probably work unseen and unheard. So it is wise to fit the door with additional bolts — perhaps mortice rack bolts near the top and bottom along the lock edge, and dog bolts on the hinge edge. (Remember though that if you provide your burglar with a choice of axes and sledgehammers in the garage it probably doesn't matter what locks and bolts you fit.)

Matchboard door

This type of door is probably unsuitable for a mortice lock, and will need a rim lock. If it is not a final exit door, add sturdy non-locking bolts.

French windows

If you can avoid it, don't use French windows as a final exit door — they are easier to protect if you can fit bolts.

The first stage is to fit bolts to the 'window' which closes first, to hold this in place as steadily as possible: it acts as the door frame for the second leaf. These bolts should be mounted vertically at the top and bottom, shooting into the head of the door frame, and into the door cill. The best type are flush bolts which fit into the door edge — the second leaf closes over these so that they cannot be seen or operated. Alternatively, fit locking surface-mounted bolts — the bigger the better.

The second leaf should also be fitted with locking bolts — either surface-mounted or mortice bolts. You can also fit a lock (you will have to if you must use the French windows as the final exit door) which will probably be a rim lock: many French windows are too thin to take a mortice lock.

If French windows open outwards the hinges are vulnerable, so fit hinge bolts at the top and bottom of each leaf as well. And if you are fitting a lock remember that outward-opening doors need a special sort.

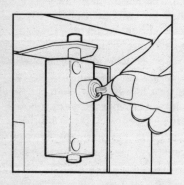

lockable bolt which locks automatically when shot, and needs a key to be opened — one way of securing French windows (ERA)

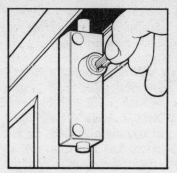

locks suitable for sliding patio
doors (ERA):

lockable bolt shooting vertically up
or down

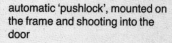

automatic 'pushlock', mounted on
the frame and shooting into the
door

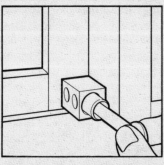

key-operated lock shooting into
the door

Patio and other sliding doors

It is wise to fit supplementary bolts to a patio door; you will
need a type specially designed for the usual aluminium-framed
doors. Fit a pair to each sliding leaf — one top left, the other

bottom right. You can get patio door locks which are key-operated from the outside — but they are unlikely to provide the security of a good door lock, and it is probably best not to be tempted by them.

A normal horizontal deadbolt will not, of course, lock a sliding door. And it is not usually practicable to fit a normal lock vertically — the door track mechanism will probably get in the way. But special sliding door locks are available which have a bolt either with a hook on the end or with claws which expand outwards as you shoot it into the staple. In either case, you are relying on the staple and perhaps the striking plate to hold the bolt against attempts to force the door, so make sure this is well fastened to the frame.

Other security features

By now, you know why two-lever locks and non-deadlockable springbolts are a bad idea. But there is more to choosing a high-security lock than simply selecting one with five levers or pins and automatic deadlocking.

British Standard

Fortunately, there is a way of being certain that a lock is going to provide more than reasonable security — look for one with the British Standard 'Kitemark' or stamped with the number BS3621.

Locks approved to the British Standard have been subject to tests simulating violent attack — trying to force the bolt back into the lock; sawing through the bolt (bolts are often made of brass, to prevent corrosion, but strengthened with hardened steel rods or ceramic layers because brass is soft and easy to cut through); drilling out vital components; and so on. The lock and any staple box with it are tested as a unit, together with the screws specified or supplied by the manufacturer. There is also a wear and tear test, simulating up to 30 years' daily use.

BS locks must have at least five levers or six pins, and may need extra anti-picking devices. The lock must also provide at least 1,000 differs.

Locks that don't carry a BS kitemark are not all bad: with

some, the manufacturer may simply not have bothered to submit the locks for approval. Others may fail only on a technicality — for example, they may provide adequate physical security, but not offer enough key differs. But at least you are sure of where you stand if you stick to BS locks.

Key registration

It is all very well locking your house up securely — but your keys need protection too. It is possible for ordinary keys to be 'borrowed' and duplicates made, the keys being returned perhaps before you even miss them. If you lose ordinary keys you always need to have your locks changed, even if all the keys are subsequently returned, in case someone has copied them when they were out of your possession.

Key registration can help. The manufacturers supply you with keys when you buy your lock, and keep details of its differ. You won't be able to get duplicates cut except by the manufacturer, and then only if you sign for them.

Many locks, one key

Installing more locks means carrying more keys, unless you buy the locks in one set and order them **keyed to pass** — which simply means that they all have the same differ, and so can all be operated by the same key.

Internal doors

There are pros and cons to locking internal doors. The argument against is that a burglar may use force to break down locked doors — and the broken doors may have more impact on you than the property stolen. And locked internal doors pose a hazard when the house is occupied: they may make it more difficult to escape if there is a fire.

The argument for locking is that a thief will want to leave as quickly as possible, and the prospect of having to spend time forcing a door (and then possibly others before finding anything worth stealing) may be enough to make him quit straight away.

Of course, the best answer is to concentrate on trying to ensure burglars can't enter in the first place. Then you can

perhaps compromise by locking internal doors only on rooms
that cannot be properly secured from outside attack. If a door
opens inwards to a room which is a likely point of entry for a
burglar, the 'for' argument is probably stronger: it is much
more difficult to break open a locked door that opens towards
you than away from you.

If you do fit locks to internal doors, they will probably be of
the mortice type, and they should be reasonably difficult to pick
(so at least three-lever or, better, five-lever). But you need not
worry so much about physical security, since the door is likely
to be weaker than the lock.

Doorstep intruders

An occupied house is uninviting to most burglars — they don't
want the added difficulty of dealing with people while trying to
ransack a house. But some burglars may be prepared to deal
with an occupant — particularly an elderly one — if by doing so
they can get into a house without wrestling with the locks and
bolts that this chapter and the next will have persuaded you to
install.

If a burglar does break in while you're at home — and
particularly if he does so with the intention of confronting and
intimidating you, rather than sneaking in and out unnoticed —
the results can be very unpleasant, to say the least. So it is well
worth taking pains to see that your home is just as secure when
you are in as when you are out — especially if you are old and
frail, and living alone.

The first precaution, but one often overlooked, is to keep
doors locked and large windows shut, even when you are in the
house. Thanks to TV advertising, many people are now
conscious of the risk of a 'sneak' burglary at night, when the
whole family is sitting around the TV, absorbed in a favourite
programme; but they are less alert to the danger during the day.
Though constantly locking and unlocking doors may be
tedious, it is important – otherwise a thief might slip into the
house and out again with a couple of easily removed possessions
while you were down the garden hanging out clothes, or
upstairs using the vacuum cleaner.

Checking out callers

Keeping doors locked whether you are in or out of the house is adequate defence against sneak thieves. But coping with callers who present themselves at the front door is another matter. How do you distinguish friend from foe? How do you prevent a foe from getting in? First, know your enemy.

● Bogus callers come in all sorts of disguises: 'officials' from the Council; gas, water or electricity workers on an 'emergency', or meter readers; solicitors and other professionals.

● They may be smart or roughly dressed; men or women; young, old or even children.

● Their real purpose may be to steal there and then, somehow keeping you quiet while they do so; or they may be aiming to find out what and how to steal from you at a later time.

Next, never admit anyone unknown until you have checked them out.

● Ask to see an identity card. If they cannot produce one, send them away.

● Check any identity card carefully. Having it flashed in front of you for half a second is not good enough; a genuine caller will happily let you handle the card and take your time to check the details on it.

● If you are still unsure, note down the details of the caller's organization; his or her name; and any phone numbers quoted. Give the card back and ask the caller to return when you have had a chance to check them out — assuming of course that you want them to. Be polite but firm; don't let them pressure, persuade, or bully you into letting them enter until you have finished your checks.

● Ring the organization they claim to represent. If at all possible, use a phone number from your own phone book (or from directory enquiries) rather than one given by the caller or on the identity card, which may be that of an accomplice.

● If you cannot satisfy yourself that the caller is genuine, phone your local police and tell them what has happened. Ask for someone to come and help you check out the caller's story.

● If the caller returns meanwhile, explain that you have had to call the police because you cannot be sure of their story: you don't need to accuse them of anything, just don't let them into the house until the police arrive.

Of course, if you have to open your front door to carry out these checks, a burglar who is prepared to use violence may be able to force his way past you and into the house. The main precaution against this are door chains and door viewers.

***

Other undesirable callers

Burglars aren't the only doorstep intruders you need to be on your guard against. Crooks of a slightly different kind include the furniture 'dealer' who may try to trick you into parting with something at well below its true value. There are variations on the straightforward theme of simply offering to buy something you don't know the value of; one is first offering an artificially high price for something you *do* know about — thereby gaining your confidence enough to be able to come back later, either to steal or to buy more valuable stuff cheaply. 'Cowboy' roofing repairers or tarmac layers need watching, too. The way to deal with these crooks is to be a good consumer: find out the normal price of whatever you're being urged to buy or sell; compare quotations from a number of people; check out trade organizations that might help; and above all don't make any deals until you are satisfied you are getting good value for money, even if it means missing out on what seems to be the bargain of a lifetime (which it very rarely will be).

***

Door chains

Perhaps the most important piece of personal security hardware is the door chain. You engage the chain when a caller comes to the door, and it allows you to open your door an inch or two but no further — so you can check out the caller before opening the door fully. Door chains are less obviously useful where the opening edge of your door is close to a wall — at the end of a narrow corridor, say — because you are unlikely to be able to see directly through the gap between the door and the frame. The trick is to fit a mirror tile to the wall.

The traditional type of chain is fixed at one end to a staple which is screwed to the door frame. The other end has a knob which runs in a metal channel screwed to the door itself. You can open the door a little bit, until the knob comes up against the end of the channel. Apart from sawing or cutting through the chain, the only way to open the door to allow access is first to shut it, then run the knob back along the channel towards the hinge side of the door, where a gap in the channel allows the knob to come out. If a caller is persistent, you may be able to persuade them that you have to close the door before you can release the chain — giving you the opportunity to lock it properly. The channel may be too long to be screwed securely to the vertical stile of the door, but on most doors it can be screwed to a rail running horizontally across the door.

Another type presents no problems on narrow-stile doors. This has the chain running through a metal loop screwed to the door, a large ring stopping it from coming out entirely. A small slot in the loop allows the chain to be freed from the door — but only when the door is closed and a special flat link in the chain can be passed through it.

A lockable door chain has the advantage that callers who have a key can let themselves in, and out again, without disturbing

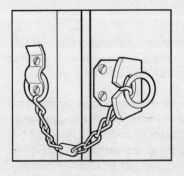

door chain suitable for doors with stiles too narrow for the channel of a traditional chain (ERA)

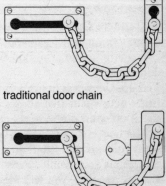

traditional door chain

door chain with lock

you or your security arrangements. This is particularly useful if you are frail and want to be sure someone can get in to help if you should fall ill or have an accident.

Checks and limiters These are names for gadgets which work in much the same way as a door chain, but usually employing a bar instead of a chain. They may give more security, especially if you are worried about the idea of someone sawing through or cutting a chain, and some types double-up as an additional bolt on the door when the door is closed.

neater and more elaborate version of the door chain (ERA)

Door viewers

If a wall next to your door prevents your getting a clear view of a caller through the gap allowed by a door chain, or if you are nervous of seeing an unknown caller face to face, you need a door viewer.

A door viewer is basically a very small peep-hole in your door fitted with a lens that allows you a very wide, although rather distorted, view of the world outside.

The lens makes it difficult for anyone outside to see *in*, but many models have a flap over the inside tube to make it completely impossible, except when you put your eye to the viewer. At night, you will need to have a light outside the door in order to see anything clearly.

Various models have different angles of view: the wider it is, the more of the scene outside your door it will take in, but the more distorted it will be, and the more difficult to recognize familiar faces. About 160° is a good compromise.

Fitting is simple: the viewer comes as two tubes which screw together, one from each side of the door, through a hole you drill in the door. The best place for a viewer is in the middle of the door's width, but some doors have only a glass or wooden panel at this point: though viewers are designed to cope with a range of door thicknesses, they are meant to be mounted in thick material and cannot be mounted in a thin panel. (You need a viewer even with a glass-panelled door if, as in most cases, the glass is not clear.) If you cannot mount a viewer in the middle, put it in one of the side rails. Fix it at normal eye-level, erring on the low side if it has to suit a number of adults. There is not much point in making it low enough for youngsters: they shouldn't be opening the door to any strangers; and a viewer placed too low will not give you a very good view of the caller's features.

door viewer seen from inside — a small peep-hole with a hinged cover (ERA)

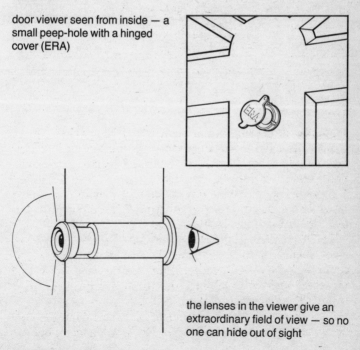

the lenses in the viewer give an extraordinary field of view — so no one can hide out of sight

Electronic aids Many modern flats have a door phone system: the outside door to the block is kept locked, and callers first have to talk to you on an intercom system linked to your door bell. There is usually an electric mechanism that then allows you to unlock the door from your flat, without having to go downstairs, if you want to let a caller in.

There is no reason why you should not copy at least the intercom part of this system in a house, so that you can look at callers through your viewer and talk to them through your intercom, without having to open the door to them at all. (If you wanted to examine their identity card, you could ask them to post it through the letter-box.)

If you fancy expensive electronic gadgetry, you could think about replacing a door viewer with a video camera set-up. Some models incorporate an intercom system and door-release mechanism as well.

6
Windows and window locks

In many households, the windows pose a more serious security risk than the doors. Anyone can see the need to have bolts or locks on doors. But non-burglars are not used to climbing in and out of windows, and it takes some imagination to appreciate the many opportunities they offer to an agile thief.

And making windows secure is not always easy — partly because so many different types are available and so many different materials are used, and partly because the size of the framework available for mounting locks is relatively small. Consequently, the range of types of lock available is confusingly large, and the security they offer varies.

As with doors, the best starting point is to understand something about your present windows — their types and construction and the faults they may suffer from. If nothing else, knowing what sort of windows you have will enable you to eliminate some items from the catalogue of window lock types that follows.

Types of window

A window usually consists of a main, relatively sturdy, framework fixed to the surrounding wall, and within that a number of other frames (**sashes**) which hold panes of glass. In most windows at least one of these other frames will be openable — hinged, sliding, or pivoting on the main frame.

Many windows are made of wood, some are of galvanized steel, and many 'replacement' windows are made of aluminium sections: these are often mounted in a wooden sub-frame.

Replacement windows may also be made of plastics.

It is easiest to look at window types from the point of view of the material used, because this probably has more effect than the method of opening on the type of locks you can use.

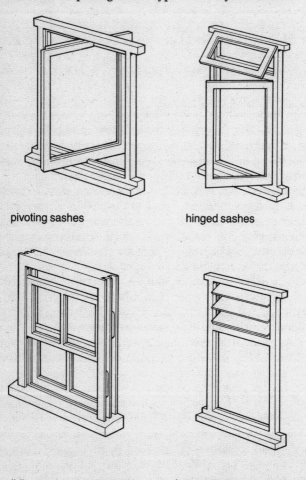

pivoting sashes   hinged sashes

sliding sashes, with weights —   louvre window, shown above a
springs are used these days   simple fixed glass pane

Wooden windows

Although windows, like doors, may be made of hardwood or softwood, the basic security of wooden windows is probably not much affected by the type of wood used — a burglar is more likely to smash the glass than bother with the frame.

Hinged sashes Probably the most commonly-used window is the wooden type with one or more hinged sashes or *casements*. These are available in all sorts of designs and sizes: they often incorporate a quite large sash hinged on the side, and a much smaller top-hinged (or 'top-hung') fan-light or vent above a fixed pane of glass. They almost always open outwards, and sit in rebates in the main frame.

Side-hung sashes are usually held closed by a pivoting catch (**cockspur** handle), which engages with a corresponding slot or peg on a **mullion** (a vertical section of the main frame, splitting the window into sections) or a **jamb** (a vertical side of the frame itself). They are usually held *open* to varying degrees with a **casement stay** — a pivoted metal bar fixed to the bottom of the sash with holes to accommodate a peg on the frame. When the sash is closed, the stay is held fast to the frame by two pegs — this can help hold the sash securely shut.

Some modern windows use a **friction stay** — an automatic holding device which holds the window open at any angle and which you don't have to manually peg in place yourself. This type of stay may also form the hinges for the sash (it draws the 'hinge' side of the sash away from the frame as the window is opened, so that you can clean the outside of the window from inside the house).

Top-hung vents usually rely on just a casement stay to hold them closed (as well as open).

Sliding sashes The design of a vertically sliding sash window is quite complex. There are usually two sashes, each running in its own channel formed in the frame jambs: the top sash, which you pull downwards to open, is mounted in the outer channel, the lower sash, which you push upwards to open, in the inner one. In older windows, the sashes are attached by cords going over pulleys at the top of each channel to weights which hang in further channels formed between the jambs and the house walls: these balance the weight of the sashes, and hold them in any position you want. In modern versions, a neater spring system may replace the cords and weights.

The usual method of holding the sashes closed is a simple catch (**fitch** catch) between the *meeting rails* (the top rail of the bottom sash and the bottom rail of the top one): as you engage the catch, it usually draws the two sashes together closing the gap at this joint, which makes it more difficult to slip in a tool at this point to force open the catch (and it helps to stop rattles). An alternative type is the **Brighton** fastener which has a threaded bolt you use to screw the two sashes to each other. Old windows may be fitted with a very simple catch that doesn't draw the two sashes together — these are often easy to open from the outside.

Pivoting sashes These can be hung either vertically or horizontally. The pivot mechanism usually incorporates a stay to keep the window open; it is held closed by a couple of cockspur handles.

The pivot is located a little way in from one edge of the sash, so that part of the sash opens outwards, like most windows, and part opens inwards. Some locks may be fittable only to the inward-opening, or to the outward-opening part; so you need to check where you intend to put the lock before you buy.

Galvanized steel windows

These windows are not much used in modern housing, but were popular some years ago. They usually have a mixture of hinged and fixed sashes, like wooden casement windows, and are usually fitted with cockspur handles and casement stays in the same way.

They can be awkward to fit locks to, partly because steel is difficult to drill and to make secure fixings to – nuts and bolts, or threaded holes in the frame may be needed – and partly because the frame sections tend to be narrow and thin, limiting the positions in which there is room for locks to be mounted or holes to be drilled.

Aluminium and plastic windows

Replacement aluminium or plastic windows can pose security problems. It is almost impossible to fit supplementary locks to plastic window frames, and only a few devices are available that you can fit successfully to aluminium frames. And in many cases the existing locks and catches are not secure enough to resist a determined attack; when buying such windows, press for reassurance on the security of the original locks, so that replacement won't be necessary.

Louvre windows

These resemble a venetian blind, with a series of horizontal glass slats, pivoted at the ends to allow more or less space between the slats for ventilation. With most types, the slats are not fixed in the metal holders at each end, but can be slid out — even when the window is closed.

Better types do have the blades glued in place (or you can do this yourself, with an epoxy resin) or come with a blade-locking device. Or you may be able to get window locks to suit.

Glass and glazing

Whatever type of window you have, it is the glass within it that is most at risk. Burglars will smash the glass so as to release catches on the inside so that they can open the window. They will rarely climb through a broken pane because of the risk of injuring themselves, particularly at night when the jagged glass edges are more difficult to see.

So small-paned windows can be as much of a risk as ones with larger panes: one small broken pane is still large enough to get an arm through. Similarly, small vents need locking just as much as larger opening sashes — though a thief might not be able to crawl through an open vent, he could use it to reach in far enough to open catches on larger sashes.

On the other hand, a large-paned fixed window might not be so vulnerable as it appears: a thief may worry that breaking it will make too much noise, and that it will take too long to clear enough space to climb through without the risk of injury.

Making glass more secure

In most cases, it is usually cheapest and easiest to accept that glass can be easily broken, and to concentrate on making the locks on the other side of the window unopenable without a key. But in some cases this is not possible, and the way to achieve security is to make the glazing itself less easily breakable. Fortunately, there are various ways of doing this, some more successful than others. (If you want your glazing to perform safety as well as security functions, ask the **Glass and Glazing Federation** — or your local GGF glass merchant — for leaflets which describe which types to use where.)

Toughened glass This is designed mainly for personal safety — if you fall against it it is much less likely to break than normal glass, and if it does break it shatters into lots of tiny fragments rather than into large jagged pieces. Because it is more difficult to break, it gives added security as well, but if a thief does break it, he will be able to climb straight through the frame without worrying about injuring himself. You have to order it cut to the right size — it cannot be worked once it has been toughened.

Wired glass This has a wire mesh sandwiched between two layers of glass. It is principally designed for fire safety: the mesh holds the glass fragments in place even if the pane is shattered by the heat of a fire, but the glass itself it just as easy to break as normal glass. Simple wired glass uses a sort of chicken-wire mesh, and this is not particularly secure against burglar attack: it is relatively easily bent out of the way once the glass has been broken (though its presence may act as a deterrent).

Georgian wired glass This is more thief-proof: the mesh consists of rather thicker metal rods, welded together, that a thief would find more tedious to cut his way through. The glass can be cut at home, but it is a job that is probably better left to a skilled glass merchant.

Laminated glass This consists of two layers of glass sandwiching a clear plastic sheet. It is the most burglar-proof type, and has safety advantages too; it *can* be broken, but the plastic layer holds the pieces of glass in place and provides another barrier that the thief would have to break through. Laminated glass can be cut at home, but this is another job better left to a skilled glass merchant. If you want fire security as well, consider laminated wired glass: its only drawback is that the minimum thickness is 9mm, because of all those layers, and this may be more than your window (or door) frame rebates can cope with.

Polycarbonate sheet A useful alternative to glass, this is a virtually unbreakable clear plastic material that stays clear (some types of plastic discolour over a period of exposure to light) and is relatively resistant to scratching. Perhaps the best way to use it is as a lining to a window that you don't want to re-glaze for some reason.

Leaded windows

Diamond-paned windows may look antique, but the real ones are a security nightmare. Each pane is held in place only by the soft lead framework that goes to make up the diamond-shaped lattice. To remove a pane, a thief can simply pull back the lead with a blade, or perhaps even a fingernail. The gap is usually big enough to get a hand through to release a catch. Fixed windows would be rather more bother: the thief would have to remove a large number of panes, then hack through the lead lattice.

A modern leaded window is usually a cheat — a standard sheet of glass with lead strips glued to its surface. So these are no extra hazard, and if security is more important than genuine appearance you could consider replacing original ones with the mock type. If you want to keep an original leaded window intact, probably the best solution would be to face it (on the inside) with a sheet of glass or (even better) polycarbonate.

Double glazing

Double glazing can help security — but it doesn't necessarily. **Sealed units** are two panes of glass in one unit with a small air-gap between, mounted in a window frame in the same way as a single sheet of glass: these are unlikely to be any more secure than single-glazing using the same sort of glass.

Secondary glazing employs a completely separate window,
usually mounted internally in the window recess. This won't
help security at all unless the secondary window is itself locked;
and most secondary window frames are aluminium which are
not the easiest type to secure (see page 75). But if both the
primary window and the secondary window are well secured,
secondary glazing is clearly going to make life doubly difficult
for anyone intent on getting them open from the outside.

Glass fixing

The alternative for a thief, instead of all this tedious messing
about with smashing glass and coping with security glazing, is
to lift the entire glass pane from its frame — which can be easier
to do than you may think. Most glass is held in place by putty
(with or without the assistance of little nails buried beneath the
surface). New putty, even putty months old, can be quite soft
and relatively easily dug out to release the pane. Very old putty
has usually cracked and broken away — though any that is still
intact is usually extremely difficult to hack out.

Modern glazing makes more use of beading strips to hold
panes in place. The glass in plastic replacement windows, for
example, is held in place with plastic or rubber seals and plastic
beading strips on the outside: with some types, the strips can be
prized off relatively easily — a point to watch out for when
buying.

Window faults

Windows are prone to the same sorts of faults as doors — see
pages 42 to 44 for details — and should be treated in much the
same ways. In particular, make sure that opening sashes fit
their surrounding frames well, and that the window as a whole
is reasonably sound before you waste time fitting a battery of
locks to it.

Though catches and casement stays on their own do not
amount to adequate security, they can make it more difficult to
force open a window that is also securely locked. So it is worth
making sure these items are in good condition and firmly fixed
in place.

Window locks described

There is such a wide range of types and patterns of window lock that it is difficult to categorize them in any helpful way: many of them will work on a variety of window types; many of them will perform a number of different functions. So they are described below in terms of how they operate, which should at least give you an idea of what will suit your particular windows and needs.

Locking bolts and catches

There are models of these to fit all sorts of windows — metal or wooden; sliding, swinging or pivoting. They all consist basically of a body holding a simple key mechanism and a sliding bolt (usually; sometimes it's a pivoting catch) plus a staple or striking plate, depending on how the lock is to be mounted, for the bolt to shoot into.

You can get bolts with combination locks (where you set a number to release the bolt); cylinder locks; or simple lever locks. Many types can be locked without using the key, which makes the business of locking up before you go out much easier — and therefore makes it more likely you will do it.

Fixing Apart from making sure that you have picked a model suitable for the material of your window, check how it is going to be fixed. If the frame pieces you are going to lock together meet flush with each other (as in the sash window example shown) you will need a box staple; if they meet at an angle, as is more likely, you will probably drill a hole in one component to take the bolt, and cover it with a striking plate. If it's a hinged window, the bolt mounts on the window; if it's sliding, the bolt must mount on the frame at right angles to the direction of sliding, or on the window with the bolt shooting vertically.

In most cases, the two parts of the device need to be fixed exactly at right angles to each other. Some windows have frame pieces with sloping faces: on these you would either have to chisel out a small area of the frame so as to cancel out the slope, or buy a lock which comes with wedges to go between the lock and the sloping frame.

Hinged staple lock One possible disadvantage of most conventional locking bolts is that the fixing screws are usually accessible. Though it would be a difficult job for a thief to unscrew a lock while leaning in through a broken window, it might be helpful on some windows to choose a version where the screws are hidden.

The design of the hinged staple lock makes this easy. The lock part (fitted to the sash if it's hinged, to the frame if it's sliding) consists of a swinging arm which you hook over a projecting bracket on the frame (or sash) when the window is closed. The bracket hides the screws in the arm mount; the arm mount hides the screws holding the bracket.

Peg lock This is a very simple type of threaded bolt that you fix to the opening sash, and a bracket that you fix to the frame. When the window is closed, the bolt pokes through a hole in the bracket, and you secure it in place with a nut; the nut is a special type that cannot be removed unless you dial the correct combination or (on other models) use the key.

Mortice rack bolts

These are the same as the ones used on doors (see page 46) except that they tend to be smaller, to suit the thinner woodwork of windows. (They can, of course, be installed only on wood windows.) They are not automatically locking, which is a slight drawback.

Handle and stay locks

Since the drawback of standard window catches is that they are not locking, the obvious answer is to make them so. Hence, you can get **locking cockspur handles** for hinged windows, and **locking fitch catches** for sliding ones.

If you do not want to replace your existing cockspur handles (or cannot — they are a permanent part of many metal windows) you could fit a **cockspur stop** instead. This works only where the catch of the handle bears on the surface of the window frame, rather than engaging in a slot within its thickness. The lock consists of a surface-mounting locking bolt that you fix vertically under the catch part of the handle. When the bolt is shot closed it stops the catch from being swung open; when it is open, there is enough clearance for the catch to move. Check that it is not possible to swing the catch *upwards* to open the window; if it is, fit another stop (perhaps no more than a length of threaded bolt) to prevent this — otherwise the cockspur stop will be useless. Some cockspur stops have a key; others are locked simply with a screw.

Casement stay locks work with your existing stays. For stays with holes you can replace one of the pins on the frame with a special one that takes a locking nut or bolt. This is likely to be practically impossible on metal windows, but you can use instead a **window stay clamp** — a metal clamp that will wrap around both the stay and its pin bracket on many styles of metal window, and which you can then hold in place with a locking pin. For window stays without holes there is a bracket which screws to the window frame underneath the stay; when the stay is closed you can lock a pin through the bracket and over the stay. Few stay locks are key-operated: most of them use screw-operated bolts (see below).

Screw-in bolts

These are simplified versions of locking bolts. One type is a **peg lock**, but without the combination lock on the nut; instead you use a special sort of key to screw the nut over its bolt.

The **dual screw** is mainly for use on sliding sashes; a threaded bolt screws through a similarly-threaded barrel fitted in the inner meeting rail until it penetrates into a staple hole drilled in the outer meeting rail. Again, the bolt can be screwed in and out only with a special key. For hinged windows there is a variation in which the barrel is surface-mounted.

Ventilation locks

Many people like to leave a window open for ventilation and at the same time make it burglar-proof. It is possible to leave a window locked but slightly open in a variety of ways:

• some cockspur handles have a notch in the catch which allows a window to be left slightly ajar; these may still be lockable with a cockspur stop bolt

• you could replace the casement stay pin which you use to hold

a window open with a locking type
● you could fit an extra locking strap to the window
● you could fit a locking pin to a sash window, with the staple positioned to hold the sash slightly open.

Whatever you use, it is really not a good idea to leave a window even slightly open when you go out: the window is then too easy to force. But ventilation locks are useful when the house is occupied — perhaps to stop children falling out as well as burglars climbing in.

Choosing locks

Deciding which locks to put on your windows is quite difficult. One device might appear ideal — until you find that your particular window frame is just the wrong shape to accommodate it, or that in its recommended position you can't reach to operate it. So the best solution is to find out what is available locally and, for each device that seems to meet your needs, go through this checklist to find the best candidate:
● reject anything that can be opened **without a key**, unless your window is fitted with laminated glass
● look for devices that **cannot be unscrewed** easily, and that use relatively **large screws**; this is particularly important for secluded windows, where a thief will be able to spend more time coaxing a lock out of its rightful place
● bolts that **automatically lock** are the most convenient to use — and so are the most likely to be used
● similarly, **single-turn key** locks are more convenient to operate than screw-down types (these also make escape from fire easier)
● devices that are **clearly visible** from outside the window might act as a deterrent (though they are usually even more clearly visible from inside, which you might not find very pleasing)
● try to fit devices employing the **same key** on all your windows — again, for convenience
● don't worry too much about key security: a thief is more likely to try smashing up a window lock than picking it; even the locks with very simple keys having no differs are probably

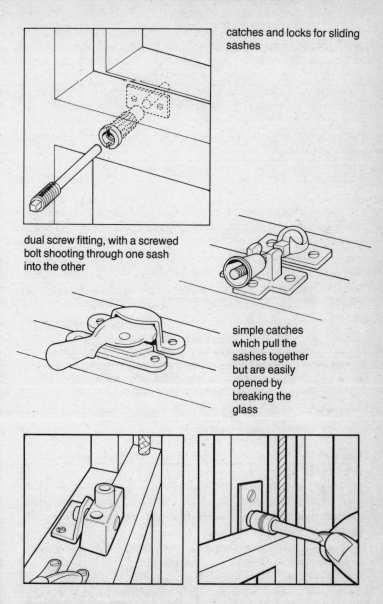

catches and locks for sliding sashes

dual screw fitting, with a screwed bolt shooting through one sash into the other

simple catches which pull the sashes together but are easily opened by breaking the glass

locking sashbolt and sashlock (ERA)

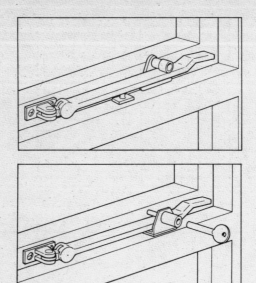

locks for casement stays: there are many different models available, to suit different types of window and stay; on this page are shown some of the possibilities, including (below right) a clamp designed to fit a metal window frame (ERA)

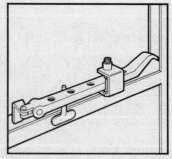

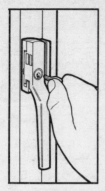
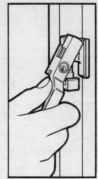

locking cockspur (ERA)

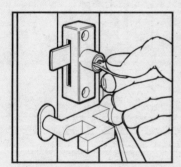

alternative ways of securing a metal window (ERA)

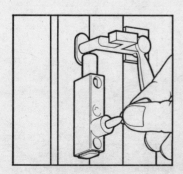
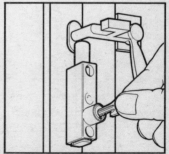

automatic locking bolts used to lock a cockspur closed (ERA)

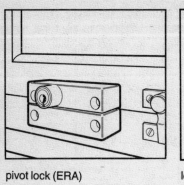

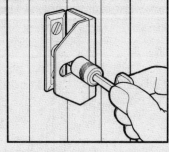

pivot lock (ERA)   locking catch (ERA)

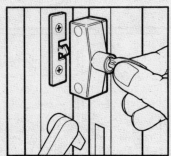

snaplock, which locks on closure and is available with simple (left) or
more complex (right) keys (ERA)

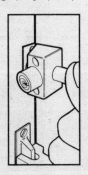

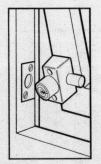

automatic locking bolt, fitted to hinged and pivoting sashes (ERA)

secure enough — the number of brands on the market effectively provides sufficient differs to make it less likely a thief will have a key to fit your particular locks
• don't forget that you may need bolts on the **hinge side** of a window, too, if (as in most cases) your windows open outwards and the hinges are vulnerable — as with doors; on traditional wooden windows you may be able to fit hinge bolts (page 48) set in mortices within the door.

Security

Few window locks are beefy enough to deter a really determined burglar, or have lock mechanisms sophisticated enough to put off a skilled one.

If you follow the tips under 'Choosing locks', above, you will be well on your way to having reasonably secure windows. If you still have a choice of devices in your local shops, go for the largest that will fit your frames comfortably, and use what appear to be the most sturdy fixing screws.

With close-fitting windows and securely mounted catches and stays you may need only one additional lock per window. To check whether you need more, try pushing your window open from the inside: you need additional locks at any point where it gives.

hinged staple lock (Yale)

7
Garden security

Making the garden and grounds of your house secure is really about three things:
● providing security for items you keep in sheds, greenhouses, garages and so on
● making sure tools and equipment that you keep outside the house — whether under cover in sheds or not — cannot be used to help a burglar force an entry to your house
● securing the grounds themselves — again, so that they hinder a burglar's entry to your house.

That means that there is quite a lot to consider when you start thinking about your garden from a burglar's point of view.

Do not make the mistake of thinking that, because the few tools you keep in a shed, garage or other outbuilding are not very valuable, there is no reason to keep the place locked. The tools may be of little value to you — but they may be very valuable to a thief who is looking for something to help him break in to the house. So secure locks and bolts may be just as worthwhile on outbuildings as on your house itself.

Your first job is the same as with your house: check that windows and doors fit properly and are in good condition. There are particular points to look out for in each case.

Windows in outbuildings

These are often broken, loose or easily removed. Sheds are often tucked out of the way, and a thief may be less inhibited about breaking a pane. Unless the panes are very small, consider glazing them with an unbreakable material. It may not need to be one of the more expensive safety glasses or poly-carbonate: the cheaper plastics will deter entry just as well, and in most windows it will not matter if the pane scratches easily, or discolours within a year or two. But whatever you use, even if it is ordinary glass, make sure it is firmly held in place and cannot be removed easily.

There is a theory that thieves are unlikely to spend time breaking into a shed or garage if they cannot tell what tools or valuables it contains. If you go along with this, use obscure glazing on your windows, or cover the insides with a translucent sticky-backed plastic (this will also make them a little more difficult to break through), or use a cheap plastics material instead of glass (and wait for it to discolour).

Do not have more opening windows than you need. Make sure those you do need to open are fitted with proper catches and stays; and screw shut those that do not need to open.

Doors in outbuildings

These are often flimsy; strengthen where you can, and at least make sure that what is there is a good fit in its frame, and provided with strong, securely fitted hinges. Then you will have to rely on sturdy bolts and catches to provide a measure (perhaps even partly an illusion) of security.

Hardware

There are two main types of locking bar which are particularly appropriate to outbuildings — though if the door is substantial enough you can fit the same sorts of lock used on house doors. Both sorts of bar employ a **padlock** to do the locking:

● a **padbolt** is like a tower bolt (see page 45) but the handle at the end of the bolt hooks round a holed metal bar that you can thread a padlock through

● a **padlock bar** or **hasp and staple** consists of a hinged plate with a slot (the hasp) that you screw to the door; when the door is closed you swing the hasp over a metal ring (the staple) screwed to the door frame; you then thread a padlock through the staple to lock the hasp in position.

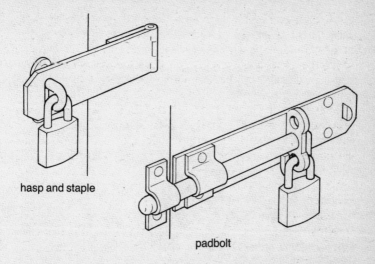

hasp and staple

padbolt

With either device, the first important thing is to make sure that it cannot easily be prized off the door or frame; the security of the padlock itself is something you can worry about later. The fixing screws should be plentiful, generous in size, and well secured into sound timber. Rusty screws become weak and loose, so use rustless ones — zinc or chrome-plated.

There are three ways you can ensure the screws themselves cannot be undone:

• use **clutch head** or **non-return** screws. These are screws which have a specially designed slot that gives the screwdriver plenty of grip when tightening the screws but no grip at all when trying to remove them

• use cross-head screws and **drill out** the cross after fixing

• use a **security locking bar** — a particular variety of padlock bar designed so that when it is locked, the hasp covers the screw heads in both itself and the staple.

Alternatively, use **carriage bolts** for fixing. These have a smooth round head with no slot; they go right through the woodwork and are secured by nuts on the inside. Just underneath the head is a square section; the holes in many locking bars are shaped to take this section and stop the bolt turning if you use the right size of bolt.

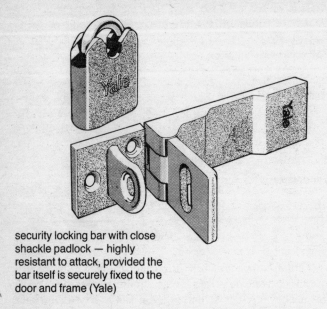

security locking bar with close
shackle padlock — highly
resistant to attack, provided the
bar itself is securely fixed to the
door and frame (Yale)

Padlocks A padlock is basically a metal ring in two parts that
are joined by a hinge at one point and a lock at the other. The
shackle of the padlock can be locked into the body to form the
complete ring, and can be swung or hinged clear so that it can
be put through the shackle of a locking bar. The lock can be
either a lever or a cylinder type; for good security the mechanism should have at least five levers or pins. It is housed in a steel
body, usually hardened to make it resistant to attack; the
keyhole is often on the underside of the body, but if it is in a
position where it is exposed to the weather it should be protected by a flap.

The shackle should also be of hardened steel. In a **close
shackle** padlock, the hole formed by the shackle and the
padlock body is made as restricted as possible, just big enough
for the locking bar's shackle to pass through. This prevents a
lever being pushed in to prize the shackles apart.

Padlocks can be self-locking (you just press the shackle home
into the body) or key-locking (you have to turn the key to hold

the shackle closed). Either way, there is still the bother of having to cope with another key — except that you can get some padlocks that are **keyed to pass** with your house locks (that is, that use the same key as all your other locks).

Garage

As well as probably providing a thief with a good source of tools, garages pose four possible security hazards in particular:
- largish windows
- a door which is certainly large, and probably weak
- possibly a concealed entrance to the house
- a tempting place to store bulky possessions — which may also be quite valuable.

Car doors

Car doors (not the ones *on* your car, but the ones you drive the car *through*) are particularly irritating from a security point of view: they must usually count as a final exit door and so be locked from outside, and securing such a big and usually lightweight door poses problems. And the last thing you want to do when you have just driven your car out of its garage, on the wettest day of the year or when you are late taking the kids to school, is to have to get out and wrestle with a large and unwieldy door.

The ultimate answer to this is to fit an electrically powered remote-control door which you can close and lock (and re-open again on your return) from inside your car — using either a key-operated switch mounted in a post alongside your drive, or a radio transmitter unit you keep in your car. Remote-control mechanisms are not cheap, but they are perhaps less expensive than you think — they cost about the same as a double up-and-over door itself.

If your door is going to remain manually operated, make sure it is properly hung, with any mechanisms correctly adjusted and lubricated, so that it is no more bother to close than necessary. Side-hung wooden doors can be a particular problem, often sagging and binding on the door frame or the drive; at least make sure they fit well, and consider having the free end supported on a castor running on the drive.

Having made the closing as easy as possible, consider next how to lock the door. This depends on whether the garage is fitted with hinged wooden doors, or the metal up-and-over door which is now more normal.

Wooden doors On double wooden doors the first leaf to close should be fitted with large barrel or tower bolts (see page 45) fitted on the inside of the top and bottom of the door, shooting into the door frame head and the garage floor. There can be two problems with this simple specification.

The bottom staple is usually no more than a hole in the concrete floor, which becomes enlarged with use, full of dirt, and quickly useless. The answer is to replace the hole with a metal staple concreted into the floor and sticking up slightly above it. Some bolts are sold with a matching staple, specially shaped to be securely fixed in concrete. The top bolt presents a difficulty only if the door has glass panels in it. In that case, you would need either to use a locking bolt or a flush bolt recessed into the door edge — more convenient to operate.

The second leaf can be locked to the first one with a dead-locking mortice lock or (more probably, as the door is not likely to be very thick) a rim lock. If you use a lock with a springbolt (as with virtually all rim locks) make sure you specify one for an outward-opening door. It makes sense to use a lock which conforms to the British Standard (see page 62).

Metal doors A metal up-and-over door can be something of a security liability: it offers a large target; it is unlikely to have been supplied with particularly secure locks; and, being made of metal, it is difficult to attach supplementary locks to.

The best solution, where possible, is to treat it as not the final exit door: fix additional bolts at all four corners on the inside of the door, and leave the garage by a personal door. If you want (or have) to lock the door from the outside, then replacement high-security locks are available, which lock a full-length bolt that shoots into the door head and the garage floor. If you think that the door could still be forced, you might be able to fit two such locks close to the sides of the door, rather than one in the middle, or perhaps mount them horizontally. But a lot depends on the design of your door and how any bolts might interfere with the opening mechanism. Arrangements like this are not likely to be direct replacements for the original locking mechanism, so alterations to the door will be needed.

An alternative, though not as convenient in use, is to fix hasps (see page 90) to both bottom corners of the door, fitting into staples concreted to the ground just outside the door.

Personal doors

Treat a personal door from the garage to the grounds as you would any house door, and fit it with a high-security lock if it is a final exit door, or bolts operated from inside if it is not. Personal doors leading from the garage to the house need special care: see page 59.

Storing possessions

A garage, particularly if it is attached to the house, is a great place to use as an overflow store from the house — in the summer, for example, when you are sorting out your camping and holiday gear, or at Christmas as somewhere to hide presents and keep the mountains of food and lakes of booze. If you have protected your garage as securely as your house, this is fine. If you haven't, you are asking for trouble.

Other outbuildings

Though your garage poses particular problems, and is the most important to secure, do not forget other outbuildings.

Shed

Shed doors are probably best secured with a locking bar, rather than a conventional mortice or even rim lock.

Greenhouse

A greenhouse is clearly highly vulnerable to break-in. And, unless you are growing valuable prize orchids, there is probably not much point in trying to make it secure. Concentrate instead on keeping it free of things worth stealing, or items that could be used to help break in to the house.

If you definitely want to secure the place, then you will have to think in terms of laminated or other safety glass; locks on opening windows and doors; and grilles over ventilators.

Porch

A porch, conservatory, or similar extension to the main building can provide you with an additional line of defence in front of a main house door. Or it can act as cover for a thief, allowing him to work at a locked door with more leisure and in more comfort.

If a porch would provide a thief with cover you should treat its outer door as a main house door; the kind of locks or bolts you fit will depend on whether the porch is your final exit or not. You may then be tempted to skimp on the security of the inner door — but, just in case you have to leave the porch open at some time, a better plan is to make the inner door as secure as the outer. And the doors and door frames on some porches are not strong enough to be trusted with the entire job of protection.

A fully glazed porch, open to view, may seem not worth locking. But it still provides another barrier: even if a thief is willing to break the glass to get into the porch, he may not be willing to do this *and* then tackle the main house door.

Securing outside equipment

Some equipment may have to be left outside, either because there is no room for it in a shed or because it is inappropriate to bring it into the house.

Long **ladders** are the prime example — just what a burglar needs to get at ill-secured upstairs windows, and very difficult to lock away in a shed or garage. You can get brackets that allow ladders to be hung on a wall and which incorporate locking bars to secure the ladder in place — though you may be able to improvise suitable arrangements more cheaply.

A **bicycle** may have to be stored outside, if you have no room for a garden shed and do not wish to share the front hall with it. You will probably already have a bicycle chain that you use to lock the machine whenever you take it out: make sure you use this at home as well. Bolt a metal hoop or bracket to the house wall, and chain your bike to this.

Securing the garden

For most households there is no sense in trying to prevent a burglar from gaining entry to the garden — a fortress approach is probably even less desirable than it is possible. What you are trying to do is to make your garden less inviting for a thief, in the hope that he will be put off even before he begins.

You do this in two, largely conflicting, ways: by putting up barriers that are difficult to pass through, perhaps psychologically rather than physically; and by removing obstructions which give a thief cover to work by. Working out the balance between these two, and at the same time keeping the garden visually acceptable, is not easy.

Fences, gates and visibility

A good compromise in most cases is to separate the front of the house from the back. A secure barrier at the side of the house does not usually look out of place, and probably will not be screening off any area where a thief might work. Use a brick wall or stout fence, and a lockable gate. The height need not be much more than a couple of metres: though any agile thief *could* climb over this, few would want to run the risk of being caught doing so.

Having done that, make sure that there is a clear view of the front door from the road, and, if possible, keep fences at the rear of the house low enough for neighbours to be able to see the back of your house — at least from their upstairs windows. A nice prickly hedge — perhaps hawthorn or, faster-growing, roses — is another compromise: once established it is a deterrent to entry even if relatively low and still leaving the house visible.

Lighting

Good external lighting not only makes it easier for you to reach your house from the road or garage (and to find your keys when you get there) but also makes life more difficult for a burglar.

Provide outside lights at all doors — on the garage as well as the house — and in any remaining vulnerable areas. Lighting the garden itself can look good as well as reducing the areas where people could lurk: even garden lighting designed mainly for visual effect, full of shadows and hints as it mostly is, can provide useful illumination.

Outside lights are not difficult to install if they are mounted on the house walls. But all electrical work has to be treated with respect, and electricity used out of doors even more so. Any light fittings you use should be clearly marked as suitable for use out of doors: ordinary interior fittings should not be used outside at all; others are suitable only for sheltered places, such as open porches. The cable you use must be armoured or otherwise protected against damage. And you should not attempt to do the wiring yourself unless you are confident that you know what you are doing.

Outside lights are an aid to security only if they are left burning during darkness. Consider your neighbours, and position the lights so that they don't cause them annoyance. You might also want to consider your electricity bill. Most outdoor light fittings are designed to take standard light bulbs or spotlights which are not very efficient and have a relatively short life. If you can find fittings which take some of the newer types of compact fluorescent bulb these will work out much less expensive to run overall — and they last much longer, so you will not have the chore of replacing the bulb so often.

Automatic lights can also reduce electricity consumption. You can have your lights connected to a photo-cell switch so that they come on at dusk and go off again at dawn; or to a proximity detector which switches the lights on only when someone approaches. See page 27.

Drainpipes

Finally, don't forget your drainpipes, which may give access to a window that you might not think to secure (though modern plastic downspouts on smooth-surfaced walls are not as attractive a proposition as old-fashioned cast iron soil stacks on an ivy-covered wall). The best answer is to secure accessible upstairs windows just as if they were at ground level. But as extra security you could paint downpipes with an **anti-climb** paint. This looks dry on the outside, but is still wet underneath its very thin skin; if you put any pressure on it, the surface breaks and so does your hand-hold.

You could also use an anti-climb paint on the top of walls, fences, porches, flat-roofed extensions and so on. But keep it away from ground level (above two metres, say) so that lawful visitors don't get covered in the stuff.

8
Alarm systems

Domestic burglar alarms are increasingly popular. But they are expensive, and before you leap to have one fitted to your house it is worthwhile considering carefully all the pros and cons. This chapter starts by doing just that, then goes on to explain the various parts of an alarm system and how they work.

Should you fit an alarm?

A burglar alarm has a different function in security from locks and bolts. It is designed not so much to keep a burglar *out*, as to tell everyone that he has got *in*. This can be useful, but it is not nearly as satisfactory as keeping him out in the first place. So the first rule is:

● do not think of an alarm system as a substitute for good locks and bolts — if you have one at all, it should be in addition to those measures.

About the only exception to this rule is when you need to keep windows unlocked for use as fire exits (see page 137). And, if you are unsure about whether to lock inside doors to provide a second line of defence, you may decide that an effective alarm system is a suitable alternative. Your insurance company may insist that you fit an alarm system if you have a lot of valuables (see Chapter 11).

So how could a burglar alarm help your security?

● A well protected house is not attractive to a thief, and the fact that you have a burglar alarm can be made very apparent: most have a large, colourful alarm box, which you can mount on the front of your house in full view. This on its own might be enough to scare off a prospective thief.

● If a thief sets off your alarm and hears it sounding (some are 'silent'; see page 120) he may judge it prudent to leave — either before he has even got into your house, or before he has had time to collect many of your possessions or do much damage.

● The sounding alarm may bring someone — you, if you are in the house, a neighbour, or the police — to the scene in time to catch the thief (or any property he might otherwise take).

● An alarm system can also provide a panic button and a smoke detector (see page 113).

But there are several possible reasons why you may think it best *not* to fit an alarm.

● It can be very expensive: even a basic system is likely to cost as much as all your door and window locks and bolts together, and complex systems can cost four times as much.

● It is even more of a nuisance to live with than locks: you have to remember to switch the system on before you go out, and switch it off when you come home. If you have it on when you are at home (overnight, say) it restricts your movements around the house considerably.

● False alarms can be a serious problem (see below).

● If you have no near neighbours, a sounding alarm will not necessarily force a thief to leave empty-handed.

A final argument often used against alarms is that having one advertises the fact that you have something worth stealing. But the opposite theory — that a visible alarm is a deterrent — is more likely to be the correct one. If you do subscribe to the advertisement theory, there is still no need to lose the other possible advantages of an alarm: just install a system in which the apparatus (in particular the bell box) is hidden from view. Then you have the protection without the high profile.

False alarms

Perhaps the major drawback of alarms is the idea that they cry wolf. An often-quoted figure is that 99 per cent of calls are false alarms. That statistic comes from a very particular source — it relates to remote-signalling (see page 120) calls from business premises to London police stations in 1983 — and it is not particularly relevant to domestic burglar alarms. But it remains a fact that the majority of alarms *are* false ones, and that they can cause serious nuisances.

If your alarm is in the habit of going off accidentally, neighbours and, more seriously, the police may give up investigating — so you lose one of the major advantages of having the system. It will also annoy the neighbours (and perhaps you). You can even be prosecuted under the Control of Pollution Act by the Environmental Health Officer.

Good design can cut the number of false alarms, or at least reduce the nuisance they cause. But by far the most important factor is careful operation: most problems are caused by people not setting the alarm properly, or forgetting that it is switched on. You have to train all the members of the household to use the alarm, and make sure there is a system which everyone will follow. Impress upon the younger members that setting the alarm off is not a joke. Be especially careful to warn visitors.

If you have an alarm system, it is essential that you tell your local Crime Prevention Officer about who can be contacted if it does go off in your absence, both to check whether there has been a break-in and to re-set the system.

Professional installation

With all the potential problems, it might seem essential to have an alarm system professionally installed. And there are advantages: a professional should know just what is needed to suit your house, your lifestyle, the particular valuables you have to protect, and your neighbourhood. Some components of a system need careful design and installation if they are to work properly. And if your insurance company demands an alarm, they will demand a professionally installed one — and specify quite closely who should install it.

But there are drawbacks: a paid-for installation does not necessarily mean a well designed and expertly installed one; but it does mean having strangers wandering about your house, legitimately finding out all about your valuables, how you live your life, and ultimately having full knowledge of your security systems. And there are scare stories of rocketing rental and maintenance costs for systems that householders cannot avoid.

You can avoid many of these problems by using a company

104 Protecting your home

that installs alarms to meet the appropriate British Standard, BS4737. This includes specifications for the components of an alarm system and how they are to be installed, and for the regular maintenance of the complete system.

There is also an inspecting body — the National Supervisory Council for Intruder Alarms (NSCIA). Companies on the NSCIA register have been vetted to ensure that they are fit to do the job (they must have been trading for some years; be able to provide a 24-hour maintenance service; and be financially and commercially sound). They must install alarms to the British Standard (BS). And they must be able to give you assurances about the integrity of any installers they use (it is not just a firm's employees you need to be careful of: check whether they sub-contract any of their work). The NSCIA carries out random inspections on new installations to make sure the installer is keeping up to the mark, and they will take up complaints from customers against firms on their register. There are also two associations of installers which operate codes of practice and formal complaints procedures, and will also recommend firms to install alarms to the BS — the British Security Industry Association (BSIA) and the Inspectors Approved Alarms Installers (IAAI).

There may be other installers in your area who do work that can be certified as complying with the BS but who are neither NSCIA-registered nor members of these associations. If your insurers are demanding an alarm, they will let you know which firms are acceptable to them. You could also ask your Crime Prevention Officer for information on local firms.

It is wise not to approach any firm until you are reasonably happy about its credentials — and it is very wise not to discuss any security matters with people selling alarms door-to-door. If you are at all interested, simply ask them to leave any literature they have and say you'll ring or call in at their office with any questions you have about their credentials before inviting a further visit.

Rent or buy? You usually have the choice of renting a professionally installed system or buying it. 'Renting', however, is not really the appropriate word: many of the components of a burglar alarm are fixed in place and most of their cost is in installation. Under a rental agreement you will own and pay for these, and pay for their installation. The expensive, easily-removable items are the only ones that you will actually rent. This means that the inital cost of a rented system, by the time you add on the first year's rental, may not be very much less than the cost of buying outright. On top of this, you are committed to a yearly rental fee. Check very carefully what the rental agreement says about how this charge is allowed to rise year by year: some agreements allow for it to double in only a couple of years.

Buying might cost only about 10 per cent more in the first year than renting a system; on the whole, buying is probably the better bet. Whether you rent or buy, there is the question of maintenance. To get NSCIA approval, the system must have a maintenance agreement in force (this used to be a BS requirement too). If it does not, you will not be able to take any complaints you have to the Council after the first year. A rented system should include maintenance in the yearly charge.

Under both the BS and NSCIA, the maintenance agreement must cover a yearly check of your system (six-monthly, if the system automatically calls the police), and some agreements may cover nothing else. Other firms may include service calls to fix faults in the system. Calls to put right accidental damage are unlikely to be covered by any agreement.

If you are buying an alarm, and not installing it to meet your insurers' requirements, a maintenance agreement may be an extra you feel you can do without (especially if you feel competent to carry out your own checks on connections, wiring and so on from time to time). But for most people the sensible course is to look for a good agreement.

Do-it-yourself

Installing your own alarm is likely to work out very much cheaper than having the job done for you. Doing it yourself is usually not difficult — on a par with wiring up a doorbell, say. It gets a bit more difficult if you are wanting to conceal all the wiring and the devices, whether for security or neatness. The amount of work involved is not trivial — perhaps a weekend plus a couple of spare evenings for a basic system.

Doing the job yourself also means that you do not have to worry about strangers — however well vetted they may be — wandering around your house legitimately learning all your security secrets. But you lose out on a professional's skill in design and installation of the more tricky components, and you do not get the protection of NSCIA. So it is unlikely that your alarm will be recognized by insurers. (There is a British Standard for do-it-yourself alarms — BS6707 — but manufacturers meeting this standard are as yet few.)

Provided you are willing and able to tackle the work yourself, don't get too carried away with over-sophisticated systems, and do not have to meet insurers' requirements, a do-it-yourself alarm can be worth thinking about: it gives you some extra protection over your lock security system without horrific cost and, because you will know in detail how it operates, you will be better placed to keep it in proper working order, and to avoid setting it off accidentally.

A compromise sometimes suggested is to buy a kit, and have someone else install it. Though this may work out at half the price of a fully professional job, it seems like the worst of both worlds: you are unlikely to get an approved firm to do such a job, so you are paying out for having inexperienced (and probably unvetted) people working on your system. And you will still get no back-up from or NSCIA.

Planning a system

Whether you design and install your own system or have the work done for you, it is necessary to understand how a burglar alarm works so that you can appreciate what protection it does and does not offer, and what restrictions it is going to place on your life.

There are four main components in a system:
● **detectors** to sense the presence of people in various ways: they may be sensitive to a door or window opening or breaking; the pressure of feet on the floor; movement within a room; or even by heat emitted by a person's body
● a **communication** system, almost always an electric cable, to

pass messages back from the detectors
• an **alarm sounder,** which is usually a bell fixed high on the
outside of the house, but is sometimes a warning telephone call
• a **control unit** to collect the signals from all the detectors and,
if you have told it to, activate the alarm sounder.

The following sections look at each of these parts of a system
in turn, explaining what they do and what is involved in
installing them.

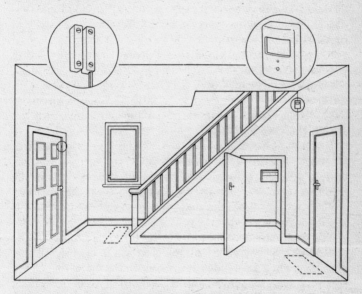

magnetic sensors (inset top left), a breaking-glass detector,
pressure mats and a movement detector (inset top right) — all
mounted in typical positions where you might fit them (though
you would never fit them all in one room); under the stairs is the
control unit

Detectors

The front line of the system is the detection devices. There are
several types, categorised here by the way in which they work;
it's also useful to distinguish 'perimeter' devices (which catch
intruders on their way in) from 'trap' devices (which catch the
intruder once inside).

Magnetic sensors

The most common form of detector is a small magnetic switch
fixed to the frame surrounding a door or opening window.
Provided the window or door is kept closed, a magnet fixed to
it, close to the switch, keeps the switch contacts held in one
position; if the window or door is opened, the contacts are
released and send a signal to the control unit.

Magnetic sensors are relatively cheap, and provide good basic
protection — making it more difficult for anyone actually to
break into your house in the first place. Fit them to all your
ground-floor opening windows and doors, and to any upstairs
windows accessible from extension roofs, drainpipes and so on.
Do not forget balcony doors, accessible skylights and so on. It
can also be worth fitting them to internal doors, especially those
linking vulnerable rooms to the rest of the house but which you
are reluctant to keep locked.

From the electrical point of view there are two sorts of
magnetic sensor. The **open-circuit** type allows electrical
current to flow through the signalling system only if the
window is opened. The **closed-circuit** type works the other way
around: current flows through the circuit until the window is
opened, when it stops.

The open-circuit type can be easier for a thief to beat: if he
can cut the wires leading to the detector, the circuit will stay
open even when the window is opened, and so the alarm will not
sound (though signalling cable is designed to make this a more
difficult job than it sounds — see page 115). Either type can be
defeated if the thief can keep the switch in the correct state with
the use of a magnet.

For these reasons, it is best to fit *recessed* sensors, fitted into
holes about 15mm deep drilled in both the opening window
sash or door and the surrounding frame. Anywhere will do, but
the further from the hinge end (on a hinged window) the better,
because this will make the detector more sensitive to small
movements of the sash. The sash should fit snugly in the frame
— otherwise the magnet may not be powerful enough to influ-
ence the switch. Fit the magnet to the sash, and the switch with
its wiring to the main frame — then you can hide the wires from

the switch in the surrounding plaster or under an architrave (this is as much to hide the position of the sensor from any interested thief as for neatness).

Surface-mounted sensors are much easier to fix: simply glue or screw them into place on the face of the frame. Since the sensor is visible (though not unduly obtrusive to a casual glance) there is no point in trying to hide the cable, so this part of the job is simpler, too. There is more scope for adjusting the two parts of the switch so that they make good magnetic contact. With metal window frames you have no choice: you will have to use surface-mounted sensors.

Breaking-glass detectors

Breaking-glass detectors are commonly used in shops to prevent burglars from simply smashing the window and helping themselves to the goods displayed inside. They are less worthwhile in houses if all your opening windows are protected by magnetic sensors, because a thief generally breaks a window not in order to climb through immediately but to enable him to open it. They may have their use on very large panes if these are vulnerable to being broken — perhaps because they are out of earshot of neighbours.

Foil strips The main type of detector consists of strips of metal foil that you stick to the face of the glass close to the edge. They are wired back to the control unit, and normally carry a current when the alarm is set. If the window breaks, the foil should break too, opening the circuit and setting off the alarm. It is not impossible for a window to be broken while the foil remains intact — and if you use the foil liberally (making such a failure less likely), your windows will start to look unpleasantly like a high-street store.

Vibration Inertia or vibration detectors are less obtrusive. They are triggered simply by jarring the window pane, and so are more sensitive than foil strip — indeed they can be too sensitive, and even heavy traffic can rattle a window enough to set one off. They are probably not suitable for a simple do-it-yourself system that you want to have maximum confidence in.

Sound detector This responds to the sound of the breaking glass, transmitted through the air to the detector, rather than direct vibrations or fracturing.

Lace wire This works similarly to window foil — a fine wire which you string all over a surface, and which will set off the alarm if it is broken by a thief smashing his way through. You would perhaps use it on a door rather than a window, and you probably need to cover it with a sheet of material such as hardboard to preserve it from accidental damage.

Pressure mats

A pressure mat is roughly the size of a door mat, but much thinner — thin enough to hide under a carpet. Within it are two sheets of metallic foil, normally spaced slightly apart; when someone steps on the mat, the foil sheets make contact and close a circuit, signalling back to the control unit. The idea is that you place a mat in front of any particularly valuable possessions — perhaps a video recorder, or the site of a safe — or in the path of anyone going from one part of the house to another.

A skilled thief may be able to spot the outline of a pressure pad (especially as he will know all the places where you are likely to put one) and circumnavigate it. They are more prone to wear than other detectors, increasing the risk of false alarms. And although a burglar may be able to avoid stepping on one, the chances are that every member of the household (especially the cat) will repeatedly step on it by accident.

So pressure mats in places such as the bottom of stairs, corridors and so on are probably not a good idea. It may just be worth using one to protect valuable possessions if you are sure you can keep pets, guests and small children out of the rooms they are in when the alarm is activated. If you install mats, check for signs of wear at least once a year.

Movement detectors

These are the most sophisticated form of detector, and more versatile than the other types. They are small wall-mounted units which 'watch' a wide area of a room and detect any movement within it. They were originally devised for large

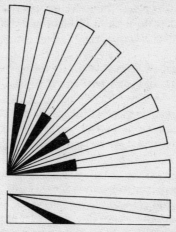

movement detectors have a wide range of view horizontally, and many are sensitive to both distant objects (shown white) and nearer ones (shown black)

commercial premises where other kinds of detector had proved inadequate.

They are less attractive in a domestic alarm system. Even though one detector might be used instead of several conventional detectors (for example, on all the doors leading off a hall) it would still be much more expensive to buy. They need careful design, positioning and setting-up to ensure that they are not likely to create false alarms, so they are probably better left out of do-it-yourself systems altogether.

In a professionally installed system, the high cost of the detectors themselves is often outweighed by savings on the installation process — with fewer detectors, there's less wiring and fixing to do. But movement detectors can be awkward if you want to set your alarm while the house is occupied (even if only by the cat), and should not automatically be included in a professional system either.

Ultrasonic and microwave With these movement detectors, a transmitter sends out a pattern of waves across a large proportion of the room, and these are reflected by the objects within it to a receiver. Provided the reflected pattern is steady, all is well. If the reflection pattern changes as a result of someone walking through the waves, the receiver sends a signal to the control unit.

Animals as well as people will upset the wave pattern of both sorts of detector, and each type can be upset by other disturbances. Ultrasonic detectors rely on air to carry the inaudible sound waves they produce, so that anything which upsets the air — such as draughts or loud noises, or even sudden changes in temperature — can set off the alarm. Microwave detectors are not affected by air disturbances, but are often more sensitive, so they can be set off by small movements, such as those of curtains in a draught. Reflective surfaces can sometimes be a problem, too. And microwave detectors can sense movement over a large area, and even through glass, thin partitions and behind furniture. Although this means that there is less chance of a burglar escaping undetected, you do have to set them up carefully so that their range is not too great — so that they do not react to birds flying past the window, for example.

Infra-red   There are two types of infra-red detector. The classic one beloved of spy films has a transmitter unit which sends out a thin beam of invisible infra-red light to a receiver: all is well so long as no one interrupts the beam. To cover a greater area, the beam is reflected from wall to wall by reflectors in a criss-cross pattern. (In the films, all you did to beat this kind of detector was to put on your infra-red specs, spot the beam, and jump athletically over it.)

The more usual type these days is the **passive infra-red** device. Unlike all the other types of movement detector, these do not send out any signals, but sense the infra-red radiation which any object, animate or inanimate, is always emitting, and register changes in the infra-red 'picture'. The aim is to detect the movement of a warm body — an intruder (though they are of course sensitive to animals as well). Early versions could also be accidentally set off by changes in other sources of infra-red heat in the area — radiant heaters heating up or cooling down, even objects warming up in sunlight — but this should not be a problem with more modern units.

Panic buttons

Panic buttons, or personal alarm switches, are detectors of quite a different sort — they are operated deliberately by the house-holder rather than accidentally by the burglar. Pressing the button triggers the alarm whether or not it is set to react to other detectors. You can use a button if you are in physical danger yourself or even if you just suspect that there is an intruder and want to scare him off. An elderly person might also find one useful for summoning help if he or she fell ill.

The two usual places for panic buttons are next to the bed, so that you can raise the alarm quickly at night, and by the front door, where you can use it if you are menaced by someone on the doorstep (though it is no substitute for a door chain or limiter: see page 66). But you could put one wherever you might find a use for it.

Because they are permanently 'live', there is a danger in placing panic buttons where they are too obvious. Not only mischievous children but even curious adults might want to play with one if they spot it. On the other hand, there is no point in hiding them away: if you need to hit a panic button, you need to be able to do so swiftly and easily.

Panic buttons are only simple switches and therefore do not add much to the cost of a system.

Smoke detectors

One advantage of a burglar alarm is that it can become the basis of a more complex system monitoring all sorts of aspects of your house. Many of the things that you could detect are hardly relevant in a domestic setting, but a smoke detector would be a useful addition — see page 134.

Perhaps the only drawback is that the more detectors you have, the greater the likelihood that one of them will set the alarm off accidentally. A compromise might be to wire an additional switch and bell into the smoke detector circuit so that it normally signals only inside the house — then if it does go off accidentally, it's only your household that suffers. If you are going away then you can switch the detector through to the main alarm sounder.

Communication

Once a detector has spotted an intruder (or thinks it has), it must send a signal back to the control unit. Almost always, this will simply be an electrical current (or the interruption of an electrical current) flowing in a thin cable.

You can connect all the detectors to the control unit separately, or you can loop several together if this would make wiring runs shorter and neater. But you have to wire closed-circuit detectors separately from open-circuit ones, unless you use special four-core cable; see below.

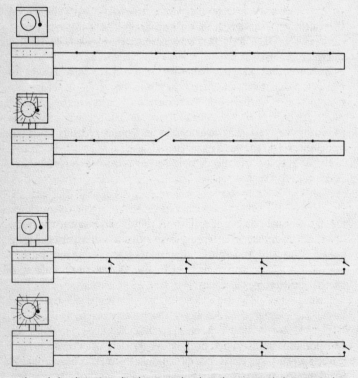

a closed circuit system (top) responds when the current is interrupted, whereas an open circuit system (bottom) responds when a current flows

Four-core cable

Ordinary two-core cable — even bell wire, as detectors work at very low voltages — can be used to wire up your detectors. But a thief has only to cut the wires (if they run to open-circuit detectors) or bridge them (if they run to closed-circuit detectors) to put the whole circuit out of operation. A much better job is done if you use special **four-core** cable.

In a four-core cable, one pair of wires forms a closed circuit; the other pair forms an open circuit (you can do this whether or not there are both types of detector on the circuit — in effect the cable becomes a special detector in itself, often called a monitor circuit). With this arrangement it is difficult for a thief to know which of the wires pairs up with which other, and which pair is the open or the closed circuit. So the chances are that an attempt to interfere with the wiring will set off the alarm. To confuse the thief even more (and you, when you are wiring up the system in the first place) the wires are not colour-coded.

Wireless control

Although cable is almost always used as the signalling method, systems are also available that use low-powered radio transmitters. You use normal detectors, but attached to each one is a very small battery-powered radio transmitter which sends a coded signal back to a receiver at the control unit. Radio transmitters are more expensive than lengths of wire, but they are much easier and quicker to install. So the system may be worth considering in a large house, or one where special care would have to be taken to hide wires, either for appearance or for security. Bear in mind the cost (and the hassle) involved in regular battery replacement.

Control unit

The control unit has a list of jobs to do:
• keep a constant check on the signals from the detectors and any monitor circuits, and activate the alarm sounder if necessary
• provide a power supply for the system

• include test facilities for checking the system, and indicators so that you know what is going on
• provide controls for setting the alarm system.
It must also possess its own security features so that it is not vulnerable to attack.

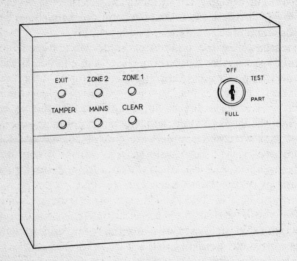

typical control panel, with lights to show what is happening and a key-operated switch

Activating the alarm

The control unit switches on the alarm sounder if a detector tells it to. To avoid creating too much of a nuisance, some units switch off the alarm after about twenty minutes, which should be long enough to attract attention. Some units then re-set the system automatically, in case a thief returns. Of course, if a detector is still sensing trouble the alarm will then sound again straight away. Some units will activate lights as well.

Power supply

A battery supply is essential so that the system is not affected by power cuts or by interference with the house electrical system.

But batteries can fail, so the better systems use a mains supply as well: this provides the power normally, and the batteries take over automatically if it fails.

If the batteries are the ordinary non-rechargeable type you should replace them frequently, whether the alarm has sounded or not, to make sure they are in good condition. Systems with rechargeable batteries avoid this chore: the batteries are kept charged up by the control unit's mains supply.

The unit should have indicators to draw attention to power supply faults: low battery power, for example (especially if the batteries are non-rechargeable) or mains failure.

Testing

When you switch on the alarm, the control unit should warn you if there are doors or windows open or other detectors in an 'alarm' condition. Some control units do this by simply sounding the alarm — *not* a good idea. The best use a small internal buzzer for this job, and have indicator lights to pin-point the offending detector. You can then carry out a **walk test**: walking around the house testing doors and windows and the other detectors until you are satisfied that they are all working and everything is closed up properly.

Setting

Once you have checked that the alarm is working correctly, you have to switch it on — and get out of the house without triggering it yourself.

Most on/off switches are operated by a simple key, so that a thief cannot easily turn off the alarm or disable the system. Others have an electronic combination lock with a keypad you tap your number on to (as you would with a cash dispensing machine).

To allow you to get out of the house without causing a false alarm, most control units have an **exit delay**: once the alarm is set, you have a minute or two in which to get out of the house, and close the door properly behind you, before the system is activated. There is a similar delay on entry, too: after opening the door you have a minute or two to reach the control unit and switch it off — whether or not you have shut the door.

Clearly, the position of the control unit must be carefully chosen. It has to be easy to reach, and close enough to your final exit door to allow you to beat the alarm. On the other hand, it must not be so close or so obvious that it gives a thief a sporting chance of overcoming the system before it sounds.

The need to get to the alarm before it sounds when you enter the house can take some getting used to. All occupants have to be trained to enter the house only by the one door on which there is an alarm delay, and to go straight to the control unit: no flicking through the post first, answering the phone, or greeting the cats. Anyone who buttonholes you on the doorstep after you've made the fateful decision to open the door must be brushed aside: however urgent their problem, dealing with your alarm comes first.

There are two alternatives to the delay system. The first is simply not to fit a detector on the final exit door. It ought to be so exposed to public view and so well secured with locks (see Chapter 5) that no thief will give it a second look. Your insurers (if they are insisting on an alarm) may not like this, but may allow you to fit a **shunt switch** — a high-security key-operated switch to turn the alarm on and off that you fit outside the final exit door. Even better is a switch built into your final exit door lock, called a **shunt lock**. With one of these, locking and unlocking the front door also switches the alarm system on and off, making an alarm system much less fuss.

The control unit should provide its own security from attack, so that the alarm sounds as soon as anyone attempts to interfere with it.

Some control panels allow you to divide the house into different areas or 'zones' – upstairs separate from downstairs, say – and to activate only some of the zones. This can be useful. If the house is divided into upstairs and downstairs zones, for example, you could keep the upstairs live while everyone was downstairs in the evening, then make the downstairs live, and perhaps shut off the upstairs, when everyone had gone to bed. The drawback of such an arrangement is that the necessary routine becomes even more complex, and following it more tedious. So the chance of people failing to stick to the rules, and so triggering false alarms, increases.

Alarm sounder

The alarm sounder is the device that actually gives the warning — either to the burglar himself and anyone else within earshot by means of a loud noise (an **audible alarm**); or to someone else via a telephone call (**remote signalling**). Or, of course, both.

Audible alarm

The most common form of alarm is a noisy bell or siren, mounted in a box on an outside wall of the house. Its purpose is to scare the thief off and to summon help. Some have a flashing light as well, which can help in two ways:

- it makes it easy to distinguish between alarms on neigbouring houses
- it can carry on flashing after an automatic cut-out has silenced the bell, so that there is some continuing indication of a break-in without the nuisance of an interminably ringing bell.

Because it is mounted outside, an alarm bell is vulnerable to attack, and so needs protecting:

- it should be mounted high up, out of reach
- its connecting wires should be run inside the house, so that they enter the alarm box from behind
- it should have tamper protection, like the control unit – so that the system cannot be rendered useless by disabling the sounder
- it can be self actuating, having its own batteries that will set off the alarm if the wires to the sounder are cut.

Internal sounder An additional alarm sounder inside the house can be useful. If it is wired to sound as soon as your final exit door is opened, without any entry delay, it will remind you to switch off the alarm system when you come in. If your system can be arranged to allow the main outside bell to be disconnected while leaving the internal sounder connected, the hazards of having the system activated at a time when the house is occupied are much reduced. The internal sounder would be enough to alert you to possible intruders without the embarrassment of bringing out half the local constabulary when, more often than not, your visitor turns out to be friend not foe.

Remote signalling

It would be rare for a domestic alarm to rely entirely on a remote signalling or *silent* alarm, as scaring off the burglar is the first objective. But if you have no near neighbours, a remote signalling device may be the only way of summoning immediate help — which is what's needed if the alarm has been set off by a panic button or smoke detector, or if an audacious burglar is relying on the alarm bell not being heard.

The simplest form of remote signalling is an **auto-dialler** system. An extra telephone line (for outgoing calls only, so that it cannot become engaged at the wrong moment) is connected to a gadget which can be set to phone any number — the police, your work, a neighbour, or 999 — and which then plays a pre-recorded message.

For greater security you could have a **direct line** connection instead of an auto-dialler connected to a normal telephone line: there is less chance of this happening to be faulty, and your call gets through instantly. But a direct line has drawbacks: it can work out very expensive; once it is installed, you cannot lightly change your mind about who the system will call. The line would be connected either to a police station (if they allow this – not all do) or to your alarm company's office (usually called a 'central station'). If you have your system connected to the alarm company, other possibilities are opened up; for example, by using a **digital communicator** rather than a simple auto-dialler, the central station can monitor your system, and can distinguish between personal attack, fire and burglary alarms. In some areas of the country, even more sophisticated forms of signalling are available, employing signals transmitted from the alarm company or the police station; these systems have the advantage that they can monitor the phone line used by the alarm, and detect any interference with it. Alarm companies and CPOs can tell you more.

If you are considering remote signalling (even a simple auto-dialler) on a do-it-yourself system, it is essential to talk to your local police before proceeding.

9
Security for valuables

Securing your home against entry is the most important step in making life difficult for the burglar, but you shouldn't stop there. Think next about how to minimize your loss if a burglar should manage to break in.

A thief will want to steal property that is high in value, small in size, or easily disposed of — and preferably all three. The items that conform to this description are the ones that you should take most precautions over. Precautions include:

- hiding valuables
- removing them from the house
- locking them up within the house
- marking them for future identification.

No hiding place

Though people may laugh at the idea of trying to hide money in the tea-caddy, or in a pot on the mantel-piece, there is some sense in the idea of keeping cash, jewellery and other valuables in unlikely places. Although there is no hiding place that is safe from thieves — not because they are skilled in knowing where to look, but because they are likely to simply keep looking in the hope of finding something, somewhere — some places are certainly more obvious than others, and more likely to be among the places a burglar will try in the limited time available to him.

So don't keep all your valuables in one or two obvious places — a locked bureau drawer, or jewellery boxes on the dressing table. Instead, put some of your possessions in other places and other rooms, tucked away in odd drawers, or unconventional places. The more places you use, and the more widely distributed around the house they are, the more likely it is that a thief will have time to discover only a few of them.

Storing things away from home

Perhaps the best way to deal with items that you do not want to use very often — your very best pearls; your will; the keys to your Spanish villa — is to get someone else to store them for you. This costs money, but you may be able to recoup at least some of the charges through lower insurance costs.

Safety deposit boxes The popular idea of a safety deposit centre is a large underground vault filled with tiers of anonymous locked boxes holding unimaginable secrets and valuables — and this is more or less true to life. Most of the high-street banks have such centres around the country, and there are other centres, mainly in London. You have your own locked box, and access to it is arranged so that no one except you knows what is in it. You usually pay according to the size of the box you hire; there may also be a charge for each visit.

When considering the hire of a box, check what hours the centre is open — some of the private ones are open until late evening and at weekends, which can be very useful for collecting and returning the family jewels for a night out.

Do not make the mistake of thinking that safety deposit boxes are invulnerable, and that you can therefore do without insurance. Find out whose responsibility it is to insure the contents of your box: if it is not yours but the centre's, check the terms and conditions carefully so that you can be sure you are getting adequate cover.

Bank safes Most people don't need the facilities of a full-blown safety deposit box, and many people do not have easy access to a deposit centre. The less romantic but more convenient alternative is just to ask your local bank to keep a deed box in their own safe to hold your papers, jewellery and so on. You pay according to the size of what you store and also for each time you take things out or put them in. You will be able to get at stored items only during bank opening hours. Again, don't forget to check on insurance arrangements.

Large items If you have paintings and furniture which constitute an unacceptable security risk at home, you could try the large auction houses. They have to store large, valuable items securely as a matter of routine, and may offer you storage.

Safes

Storing valuables in a safe is not a guarantee of security. But, like other home security measures, a safe is meant to make life more difficult for a thief by giving him another barrier to overcome before he gets what he wants. A safe can also give protection against fire, so you can use it to protect items that may not be particularly attractive to a thief but which would be expensive or tedious for you to replace — wills, share certificates and other documents, computer discs containing precious data, treasured photographs or home videos.

Before you decide a home safe is the best place for your valuables, remember that it would almost certainly be safer to store them in a bank or safety deposit box. Buying and installing a really secure home safe might cost as much as renting space in a bank safe for ten years. A key factor in weighing up the alternatives is how often you expect to want access to your valuables. It may be inconvenient to have to travel to the bank every time you want access to your safe, and if you are charged access frequent visits will make a home safe look more economically attractive. Of course, there is nothing to stop you storing some items at the bank and some in a home safe.

No safe is safe if you don't keep proper care of the keys — which means always on your person, and not labelled in any way. A combination lock (which opens only when a secret sequence of numbers is entered via a dial or keypad) is more convenient, and can be just as safe providing you don't write down the combination in any form that might be recognized.

Safes come in three types: free-standing, wall-mounted, or underfloor.

Free-standing safes

A free-standing safe — a massive metal cupboard, bristling with rivets and dials and levers — is what most people imagine when they think of a safe. By their nature, free-standing safes are big, and they can be useful if you have a lot of bulky valuables to store; but they are expensive, and you may have difficulty finding anywhere sensible in a house to put one — as much from the aesthetic as the security point of view.

The problem with a free-standing safe is not so much that it is likely to be 'cracked' in your home, but that it might be carried away by a thief to a place where he will have the equipment and the time to take it apart. Even if your original burglar is the normal opportunist type, lacking the resources to haul away a heavy safe, if he spots your safe he or his more experienced friends may come again, better prepared.

Making a safe safer Even a safe weighing a quarter of a ton, which might seem very heavy to you, is movable with the aid of enough people: if a safe can be carried into your house without much specialized equipment, the chances are it can be carried out again in much the same way. So a free-standing safe must either be very heavy — anything up to a ton, which would be extremely expensive, and might be too heavy for your floor — or be fixed firmly to the floor.

A safe could be fixed to the floor by bolts passing through holes drilled in its bottom, or by wrapping steel bands over it, and bolting these to the floor. Bolting through holes in the safe bottom is probably the better method, because the fixings are then entirely hidden in and under the safe itself. Either method will work on either concrete or timber floors: on timber ones, make sure the fastenings are secured to the joists, not just the floorboards.

You can protect a safe still further by building it into a solid enclosure. Brickwork (using a strong mortar mix) might be better than nothing — it would certainly slow a thief down. But only reinforced concrete cast around the sides and back, with the safe sitting on a concrete floor, would give serious protection from attack.

Where to put it In commercial premises, safes are often put in full view of passers-by, the theory being that a burglar would not want to attempt safe-cracking in those circumstances. But this is probably not an arrangement you would want in your own house, even if you could achieve it. The best site is in a corner, where a thief will have difficulty moving or attacking the safe. Be wary of putting even a 'light' 200-pound safe on a wooden floor without getting expert assurance that the floor will stand the load.

Buying second-hand Second-hand safes have obvious attractions — they can often be found going for a song in country auction rooms. But there are important drawbacks. Very old safes are not actually very safe: look for one where the sides, and preferably back too, are made from one piece of metal wrapped into a box shape, rather than one where the panels are riveted to each other along the edges.

Weight is clearly a problem: if a safe is light enough for you to be able to get it transported home easily, it will need securely fixing in place once it's there. Keys are also a problem: various people concerned with the sale of the safe may have had the opportunity to steal or copy a key, so you would need either to conceal the eventual destination of the safe you were buying or (for complete peace of mind) to have the lock mechanism changed after you had bought it.

Wall safes

Wall safes are designed to be built into the masonry of the house, and so need not be massive; and in practice they are quite small and light — often no bigger than a couple of bricks. Their weakness is that only a small amount of demolition work is necessary to remove the safe, which can then be carried away and taken apart elsewhere. Clearly, the safe must as far as possible be securely fixed in place. But it is also worth choosing the location carefully to cut down the chance of a thief's discovering the safe in the first place. In the films, wall safes are always to be found behind oil paintings; as burglars watch films too, it's worth trying to find a more imaginative hiding place for your safe if you can.

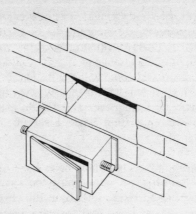

wall safe, with screws which go into the surrounding masonry

Choosing Decide first what you want to put into your safe. Don't get carried away: wall safes will not hold much; some are hardly big enough to hold a passport. When you go to buy the safe, it's sensible to take with you replicas of what you intend to store — envelopes with the same size and number of sheets of paper; empty jewellery cases; blank computer discs and so on. Although manufacturers' literature may quote the internal dimensions of their safes, it may not tell you, for example, how locks protrude into the space, or whether the door restricts the size of objects you can get into the safe.

The smallest safes are designed to fit within a single thickness of modern brick or block walling, such as the inner leaf of a cavity wall. Some are rather deeper, and are designed to protrude into the cavity of a cavity wall; it is not a good idea to reduce the width of the cavity in this way, as it could possibly lead to problems with damp. Others are much deeper and it is usually suggested that these be mounted in chimney breasts (not where it would penetrate the flue, of course, unless you are sure the flue is not going to be used again).

Fixing For fixing a safe, you need a masonry wall, not a hollow partition made of plasterboard or other sheet material. The existing construction must be sound (walls in older houses can be surprisingly frail), and if any of it is weakened as you form the opening, these sections must also be removed and rebuilt. Once you have an opening surrounded by sound brickwork which would not be easy to attack, the safe must be fixed securely to it. Some wall safes come with relatively mean lugs for fixing; ones equipped with bolts which you drive into the brickwork itself can be more securely fixed (again, assuming that the brickwork can take this treatment).

Underfloor safes

Underfloor safes are designed to be built into a solid concrete floor. With a small and very strong lid at the top giving access to a larger space within, such a safe can be the ultimate in home security when properly set in a reinforced concrete floor — very difficult to break into and almost impossible to remove.

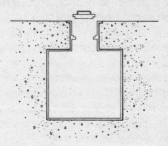

underfloor safe installed in the most secure way, surrounded by concrete; this is quite a large safe — smaller ones are available where the body of the safe and the hole at the top are of similar dimensions

To fit a safe in an existing floor you first have to cut a hole out of the existing concrete (doing this will give you some idea of how difficult it will be to remove your safe once it's fitted) and probably through into the rubble beneath. Make the hole a generous size compared with the safe. Be warned that making such a hole in an existing floor is likely to interfere with the damp-proofing arrangements, which will have to be repaired with great care. Set the safe in a strong concrete mix poured under, around, and on top of it. For the best protection, reinforce the concrete around the safe with strong metal mesh or bars.

You could site a safe wherever there is a suitable floor. But it is wise to avoid rooms where the floor gets wet; and to avoid inconvenient positions which might discourage use of the safe. In a room with a tiled floor or fitted carpet, some ingenuity may be needed to disguise the safe: you might need to provide a little separate trapdoor above the safe, which need not be too obvious if you can hide it behind or under furniture.

Security marking

There are two good reasons for marking valuables in a permanent way so that they are identifiably yours. First, it increases the possibility of stolen property being returned to you if it is recovered by the police — they have large amounts of property that cannot be returned to its owners because they have never been identified. Possessions of sentimental value cannot be adequately covered by insurance, so this is particularly relevant to them.

The second reason is that marking can (depending on how you do it) make the object less attractive to thieves in the first place. One of the reasons that video recorders and cameras are high on burglars' shopping lists is that they can easily be disposed of because they all look more or less the same. After they have changed hands once or twice, it becomes difficult to prove that they don't belong to the person who possesses them. If they are uniquely marked, there is more of a chance of their true ownership being traced — and they become less marketable and so less worth the risk of stealing in the first place.

Many expensive pieces of household equipment already bear a plate carrying the machine's unique serial number — but this never seems to put thieves off. Partly, this is because householders rarely record their serial numbers (see page 151). Partly, it is because the plate carrying the number can be removed without great difficulty or even changed for another — perhaps one taken from another machine, or simply a false one – if those selling-on the equipment think it worthwhile.

What to mark

The idea of a marking system is to enable the police to track you down if they recover goods stolen from you. But a full address would make marking hard work, and would be tricky to fit on to small valuables.

There is a police **property marking scheme** which encourages the use of an easy-to-understand code instead. It simply consists of your postcode followed by the number of your house, if it is numbered, or the first few letters of its name. Since each postcode covers only around 15 addresses, this will be enough in almost every case for the police to know exactly where any recovered property rightfully belongs.

If you do not know your postcode, and cannot find it out from documents such as a vehicle or TV licence or rates demand, ask at a post office or library for a postcode directory of your area, and look it up there.

If you legitimately sell any marked items, do not forget to tell the new owner where and how you have marked them.

How to mark

You can mark items yourself, or your local police force may be running a campaign offering to mark certain items for you.

There are two schools of thought on how marking should be done. One suggests that you should make the mark obvious, so that it acts as a deterrent to thieves. Others say that this allows the thief an opportunity to remove the mark, and that a better plan is to hide it so that your property will be more permanently traceable.

The two main methods of marking reflect each of these philosophies — a permanent and visible **engraving** which will not be easy to remove, or an **invisible marking** which will not be easy to detect.

Engraving You can do this yourself, with a small hobbyist's engraving tool, or you could ask a trustworthy jeweller to do it for you. It is suitable for functional items such as cameras or binoculars, but not for antiques or valuable silver items, for example — it would reduce their value.

Large metal items, such as tools and bicycles, may be more easily marked with a punching set (ask at an ironmongers, engineering works or blacksmiths, or even your police station, if they have been involved in a marking scheme).

Invisible marking You can buy special security pens in most stationery shops. They produce a visible mark when you write, but when the ink dries it becomes invisible, except when examined under ultra-violet light.

Perhaps the main advantage of invisible marking is that it is less destructive of your property than engraving — but you should still take advice before you use it on your precious antiques. An ultra-violet lamp is not difficult to buy, so you will not be hiding your mark from a thief very successfully. And the mark fades, particularly if it is exposed to sunlight, or if the item is washed. You should renew it every six months or so.

Flaunt it

Marking your valuables is only half the job. If you want the system to act as a deterrent to theft, as well as a method of getting your stolen property back, you need to advertise the fact that your property is marked — whether with visible engraving or invisible marking.

Security pens often come with a window sticker to make it clear to potential burglars what they are up against. Your local police may also have stickers.

10
Fire safety

It is a sad fact that you can often improve one aspect of your life only at the expense of another, and this is certainly true of home security. At the least, improved security usually means decreased convenience. More importantly, by keeping burglars firmly *out* of your house, you may be trapping yourself equally firmly *in* — so when you consider burglary security, you must also consider fire security. The idea is to balance the one risk against the other, so that your combined protection against both hazards is as good as possible. There are two main approaches: one is to reduce the risk of a fire starting, or going undetected and becoming uncontrollable. The second is to make escape from a fire as easy as possible without having to relax your burglary security precautions too much.

If you are not sure what specific fire risks there may be in your home you can call in a Fire Prevention (or Protection, or Safety) Officer from the nearest fire service headquarters (you'll find it in the phone book).

Preventing fires

Fires usually start because people are careless. The precautions you can take are well known, but they bear reiterating.

Electricity

Fires can be caused by electrical faults in wiring, more often than in appliances. Bear the following points in mind.
● Do not wire up plugs unless you know you are competent to do so; and make sure you do the job properly: wires securely

fixed to the correct terminals; cord-grip doing its job properly; right type of fuse fitted.

• Everyone is capable of spotting major faults in flexes and plugs, even if they cannot put defects right themselves. Look for frayed or kinked flexes; damaged plugs; anything held together with insulating tape; sockets sporting more than one adaptor; flexes run under carpets; plugs on high-power appliances getting warm.

• Have your house wiring checked every five years or so, and get it surveyed before you buy a house: a surveyor's report will not normally cover house wiring unless you ask specifically for it. The problem with this advice is that it is not easy to be certain you are getting a wholly unbiased report, as anyone checking your wiring will be in the business of installing new wiring too. In particular, it is best to be a little wary of anyone offering 'free' wiring inspections, and you might consider hiring an electrician on the clear understanding that any necessary work will be done by someone else. In any case, it is wise to use a firm on the roll of the National Inspection Council for Electrical Installation Contracting (NICEIC).

• With older televisions there is a chance of faults leading to fires even when the set is switched off. For peace of mind, at least, it is worth unplugging these when not in use, or at least switching them off at the socket.

• Avoid the use of multi-plug adapters whenever you can.

Gas

In a sense, gas poses fewer problems than electricity; for one thing, the laws governing gas installations require work to be undertaken by a competent person — use an installer registered with CORGI (Confederation for the Registration of Gas Installers) for any service or installation work. Treat any smell of gas seriously — it could be the prelude to an explosion:

• extinguish all flames, including pilot lights (check as you do so if any are already out) and cigarettes; but don't operate any electrical switches — you might cause a spark
• open doors and windows
• check for a turned-on gas tap or a blown-out pilot light before assuming there is a leak

• if the smell persists and you conclude there is a leak, turn the gas supply off at the meter and call your local gas region. If the smell persists after you have turned off at the meter, impress on your gas region that it is an emergency. Numbers to ring are in the phone book under 'Gas', and may be displayed near your gas meter.

Turn the gas off at the meter before going on holiday, and on your return check carefully for any sniff of a leak.

Appliances

Open and portable fires Open fires should be properly guarded all the time they are alight. Never use anything like paraffin to light a fire, or try to get it to draw by holding a sheet of newspaper in front of it. Chimneys need sweeping every two years at least, and certainly before being put into use after longer than a summer's break.

Throw away ancient heaters of any sort: paraffin ones do not have an automatic safety cut-out; electric ones are not well guarded. And never carry or refill a heater when lit.

When changing Calor gas and other liquified petroleum gas cylinders, be sure that there are no flames or working electrical appliances nearby.

Do not dry clothes around any form of radiant heater or fire.

Cookers Cooking appliances are the biggest single source of domestic fires. So:
• beware of fat that is smoking – it may burst into flames
• never fill chip pans more than a third full.
• make sure burners are turned off after use
• wear close-fitting clothing when using a gas cooker
• don't leave tea-towels to dry above a cooker
• on a window close to a cooker use blinds, not curtains
• beware of draughts wherever a window is sited
• keep electric flexes clear of cooker rings and burners.

Smoking

Because smoking involves the use of naked flames all over the house, it is dangerous. If you have smokers in your house, make sure the place is littered with ashtrays, so there is always somewhere safe for them to stub out burning materials. Make sure matches and lighters are kept out of the way of children — a third of the children who die in fires each year do so in fires they have started while playing with matches.

There are two other specific fire dangers. Modern sofas and armchairs containing polyurethane foam can produce toxic fumes that kill long before flames would. Be especially careful not to drop lighted cigarettes down the sides of furniture; and double-check before going to bed. Don't smoke in bed — you can easily fall asleep while doing so.

Foam used in furniture on sale from March 1989 has to be a special 'combustion-modified' type, which is much safer than older foams. And furniture fabrics used from March 1990 have to pass a test showing that they will not burst into flames on contact with a lighted cigarette.

Fire alarms

If you are unlucky enough to have a fire start in your house, you have no time to lose: once it has a hold, fire can spread with remarkable speed. A fire alarm — or rather a **smoke detector** — can alert you to a fire before it gets out of control, giving you time to put it out or (more important) to evacuate the house. Smoke detectors are relatively small and unobtrusive items which you fit to the ceiling; they may be self-contained or a part of your burglar alarm system.

Choosing alarms

Types There are two different types of smoke detector mechanism. The more common is the **ionization** type: a small radioactive source ionizes the air and allows a small electric current to flow; the presence of smoke changes the degree of ionization and so triggers the alarm. This type reacts best to a hot blazing fire.

Less common is the **photoelectric** type: here smoke entering the unit scatters a light beam which is being monitored by a photocell, and so triggers the alarm. This type works more quickly in a smouldering type of fire.

As you can't tell which sort of fire you are likely to have, it is difficult to say which type of detector you should go for. A few models have both detectors in the one unit. It is worth looking for a detector made to the British Standard (BS5446).

Features Smoke detectors are often self-contained, each with its own battery and siren. In a larger house, or if you keep all the internal doors shut, you might not be able to hear every alarm from every part of the house — so some models can be wired together, so that triggering one unit sets off the siren on all the units in the house.

Some units include a battery-powered light, which could help you find your way out of the house in the dark or smoke (and there is no fire without smoke).

If you have a burglar alarm system, this can incorporate smoke detectors. These may well cost *more* than self-contained units, but having an alarm which sounds outside the house could be helpful if the house is unoccupied.

Where to install

Detectors can be fooled by steam, and react too quickly to cooking fumes. So neither the bathroom nor the kitchen is a good spot to install one. In a small house, one detector in the hall plus another on the landing should give sufficient coverage.

In a larger house you will need more detectors, so that a fire can be spotted before it has grown too large. And if you shut internal doors at night (see below) a detector in each room is the only way to be sure of protection.

Checking

A smoke detector needs regular checking:
● you can test that the alarm sounder works by pressing the unit's own test button: do this once a month; to check that the detector as a whole works, hold a lighted cigarette beneath it
● failure may be due to an exhausted or defective battery; but most models automatically sound a warning bleep if battery power is low
● make sure you use the right sort of battery, and replace it at least once a year, whether it is failing or not
● keep the grille clean.

Controlling fire

When a fire is discovered, your priority should always be to get yourself and the other occupants of the house to safety, then to call the fire brigade. Tackling the fire yourself, like tackling a burglar, is a risky business. But provided a fire is small, you may be able to deal with it.

A **fire extinguisher** can be useful for tackling many fires, particularly if you live in a country area and the fire brigade may take some time to reach you. The main problem is that there are many different sorts of extinguisher, each best at tackling different sorts of fires. The last thing you want when faced with a fire is to have to work out what extinguisher to use, so a **multi-purpose powder** extinguisher (sometimes labelled ABC, and colour-coded blue) is probably the best sort. It makes a mess, but that is not something you should worry about when lives may be at stake; and it is not best at cooling fires, so they may re-ignite. But it is suitable for most types of fire, including those involving electrical appliances and wiring.

Extinguishers should be made to BS5423: to confirm that they have been tested and approved to this standard, look also for a BS Kitemark, or approval marks from British Approvals for Fire Equipment (BAFE).

With a **chip-pan fire** the important thing is the don'ts: *don't* move the pan, or try to carry it outside; *don't* use water or fire extinguishers. The only thing you can do is to smother the flames as quickly as possible: drop a lid over the pan; or use a proper fire blanket (made to BS6575), which you should keep in a proper wall-mounted container close to the cooker. When you can, turn off the heat. Do not remove the cover, or touch the pan, for at least half an hour: it could still be hot enough to re-ignite on exposure to air.

Burning modern **upholstery** is best left alone, because of the dangers of fumes and a sudden flare-up. But you could tackle it with water or a fire extinguisher.

Fires involving **bottled gas** are particularly worrying because of the risk of explosion. Unless you are sure you can safely get to the cylinder to turn the gas off, simply keep clear and tell the fire brigade there is a bottled gas fire.

Closed **doors** can prevent the spread of fire. So close all internal doors before going to bed; if you retreat from a room on fire, close the door after you. And never go into a room to investigate a fire if the door feels hot — the fire is too far gone for you to be able to tackle it.

Getting out

Many people are most worried about a fire happening at night, and rightly: even if you are woken by the fire, precious minutes will already have been lost; there is the darkness to contend with; and if you have followed the advice given earlier in this book, the house will be firmly locked up.

A smoke detector will alert you to the danger quickly, and one equipped with emergency lights may make it easier for you to see your way out (though smoke will be blinding whatever the light conditions). What remains is to consider how you can modify your burglar-proofing provisions so that you can easily get out.

Escape routes

The first step is to identify how you would get out of the house in case of a fire — your exit routes. The most normal one would be out of the nearest door; for a fire at night, this would usually mean down the stairs and out of the front door. Often a fire at night blocks the stair-well, and then the alternative route is through an upstairs window; with luck, one giving access to a bay window or single-storey extension roof. If you are in any doubt about the best escape routes — perhaps because your house has a complicated layout — get advice from your fire brigade (see page 131).

Front door This is probably your normal final exit door, which you lock from outside when leaving the house, and probably from inside to secure it at night. This is dangerous: even if you can hang a key in a safe but easily accessible place at night, finding it in the smoke and dark and then trying to insert it in a door lock is going to waste precious time. The best plan would be not to lock the door, but to provide it instead with ordinary bolts (see page 45) top and bottom — easy to find and quick to open in an emergency.

With a glazed or thin wood-panelled door you are certainly reducing your burglary security by doing without locks at night. If you are worried by this, think about installing a burglar alarm to cover this door (and any other openings where you reduce your burglary security to make a fire exit easier). Or change the door.

Upstairs window Any upstairs window which is useful as a fire exit should be lockable, because it would also be useful as a burglary entrance. So, again, for fire safety provide it also with non-locking bolts and use only these at night.

Other upstairs windows are unlikely to be lockable, and can be very useful as fire exits. Many modern houses are low enough for an adult to scramble down from a first-floor window without suffering much damage. In a taller house, you could provide the most likely exit window with a securely fixed rope ladder – or, better still, a fold-away ladder.

If secondary double-glazing is fitted to windows which might form part of an escape route, the secondary panes should be easily openable, not fixed in place.

If you are trapped upstairs, go into a room facing the street and shut the door. Block the gap underneath with a blanket or sheet, soaked in water if possible. If you cannot manage the drop from the window, open it (or break it) and shout for help.

Breaking glass Burglars like to break small window panes in order to get to the catches securing larger opening sashes. They are not so keen on smashing large panes in order to climb through directly. With a fire close behind, you are going to be less timid. So large-paned windows can act as a useful combined fire exit and burglar deterrent. If you have to smash a pane, do so with a tool or piece of furniture. Wrap your hand in a thick cloth and break off as much of the remaining glass as possible. Pad the bottom edge of the frame with another cloth, rug or whatever before trying to climb through.

If you have installed security glass in a window (see page 76) your exit through it will certainly be hampered, and if the glass you have used is any good at its job your exit will be prevented altogether. Bear this in mind before deciding that security glass is the sensible way to make a window secure against burglary — there may be other ways with less pronounced drawbacks. And if you go ahead, make sure the whole household knows which windows are no longer useful for escape.

Fire drill

Panic is a major problem in fires. If everyone knows what to do, and how they can get out of the house no matter where the fire is, they will be able to act more quickly and calmly. Though it may sound unnecessarily formal, it would be no bad idea to hold fire drills from time to time: youngsters will love it.

Keep the ideas as simple as possible — make sure everyone knows there will always be one safe downstairs exit route and one upstairs exit route. You can devise alternatives for yourself, or to share with the older members of the family.

Don't forget that your fire escape arrangements will need to be explained to anyone who you leave in charge of the house. And when you have visitors remember that your normal plan of evacuation may not be reliable if they are very young or infirm.

11
Insurance

Insuring your possessions will not make them any less liable to being stolen. It will help to lessen the shock if they are — but only if your policy gives all the cover you need. Proper insurance will compensate for the cost of replacing your belongings and making good any damage caused. But if they had to claim on their insurance some people would find that it was less comprehensive than they would like. This chapter explains how you can avoid that additional shock.

Insurance explained

Insurance is a way of spreading the burden of misfortune so that each individual finds it bearable. Instead of running the risk of a serious loss at some time in the future, you accept the certainty of paying a much smaller amount every year (called the **premium**). The insurance **policy** sets out the terms and conditions on which your insurance company agrees to recompense you for losses. The complex detail of these terms can cause problems when you try to claim: your insurers will probably have been a lot more careful in drawing them up than you will have been in reading them.

If you had a burglary, it would normally be your **house contents insurance** policy that you would claim on. But some of the things a burglar might steal and, more important, some of the damage he might do in the process, would be covered under **house buildings insurance**. This chapter looks at both main insurances in turn, explaining what types of each are available, and the cover they give. The following chapter looks at how to go about claiming, if you ever have to.

This chapter deals with insurance cover only for burglaries, but of course most insurance policies also cover loss or damage due to many other causes (or 'perils' in insurance jargon) including fire, flood, and things falling from aeroplanes, to name just a few. And there are types of cover that would not be relevant to a burglary claim, and so are not mentioned here.

House contents insurance

There are various types of house contents insurance, depending on how the policy calculates what to pay out when you make a claim (mainly **indemnity** or **new-for-old**, or a **hybrid** of the two); and how it limits what you are covered for (**all-risks**, or **insured-perils-only**). All-risks policies generally pay out on a new-for-old basis; insured-perils-only policies may use any one of the three ways of calculating payment — indemnity, new-for-old, or hybrid.

Indemnity

The intention of an indemnity policy is to put you back exactly where you were before the loss or damage — as far as possible. So for items that were stolen, you would get only the cost of replacing them with things of similar age and in similar condition, worked out in the following manner:

● for items which do not decline in value over their life (or items like antiques, which actually become worth more as years go by) you get the full cost of buying a replacement

● for items which do depreciate, you get only the fraction of the replacement cost that corresponds to their remaining life — if the item is three-quarters of the way through its life, for example, you get a quarter of the cost.

In principle, you might hope to find second-hand replacements for the belongings you have lost, and pay out something like what the insurance company pays you. In practice, this is normally difficult and often impossible, and you would be likely to replace old possessions with new ones. You end up with something better (or, at least, newer) but you do have to pay towards the cost. You may be prepared to accept indemnity cover for many items: you may not mind having to pay the extra to buy a new stereo, for example. And you may be positively delighted to settle for half the cost of a five-year-old TV that you now never watch. But there is a danger with indemnity insurance that a major burglary (or, even worse, a serious fire) could leave you facing big bills or a much reduced standard of living, and most people prefer new-for-old cover.

New-for-old

A new-for-old policy is more generous in its pay-out. You get the full cost of repairing items or replacing them with their new equivalents, and with no deduction for wear and tear. Of course, new-for-old costs more, too. When expressed in terms of what you pay per £1,000 of cover, new-for-old looks only slightly more expensive than indemnity cover. But you have to buy a larger amount of cover, so the premium you pay will go up in proportion.

Whether it is worth having depends on how you view your belongings. If you must have all the items that you currently possess, and would not be able (or want) to pay the difference between their current value and the cost of replacements, new-for-old is what you need. It may be more attractive if your possessions are fairly elderly — because your share of the bill for replacement would be proportionately higher. If you are very unlucky, and suffer a total loss of your belongings, new-for-old cover will prove very worthwhile.

Any new-for-old cover excludes sheets, blankets and other 'linen', and also clothes — you get only indemnity cover.

Hybrid

This is a compromise policy: new-for-old cover on items under a certain age — either all of them, or just things like furniture, carpets, and most 'brown goods' (radio, hi-fi, TV and so on) — and indemnity cover on the rest.

Insured-perils-only

This is the most common form of policy: you are insured only for the risks ('perils') actually mentioned in the policy, which will be modified by restrictions (called 'exclusions'). These should be studied closely so that you understand fully the extent of cover provided. It is relatively cheap, but it may leave you uninsured without realising it, because it is often difficult to work out what is and is not covered in your particular situation.

A basic policy will usually pay out for loss or damage (so far as theft is concerned) in the circumstances listed below. The exclusions given are typical ones, but policies vary considerably in the cover they provide.

The objects covered as 'belongings' generally include furniture; clothes; valuables; money; tools; documents; domestic equipment; 'brown goods' (TVs etc); and other items which are usually kept in the house, garage or outbuildings. Cover does not usually include:

● anything that is fixed in place (so a free-standing wardrobe is belongings; a built-in one is not)

● anything that is normally kept in the garden (so house-plants may be covered even if they are temporarily sitting on the patio; plants growing in the border will not be)

● garden furniture in excess of a specified limit, when it is left outside

● cars and accessories.

Theft from your home, garage or outbuildings (or attempted theft) of your belongings, but not:

● if your home is not self-contained or if there are other people living in your home that the insurers do not know about (whether they may have been responsible for the theft or not), unless the thief had to force his way into or out of your house

● if your home is sub-let or even while it is lent (to friends, say), unless the thief had to force his way into or out of your house

● by members of your family

● if the removal of your possessions 'involves deception', or if you have let the burglar on to the premises

● loss of money, unless the thief had to force his way into or out of your house; 'money' may include things like travellers cheques, travel tickets, stamps, postal orders and so on

● loss of documents, certificates and valuables, and money

again, worth more than certain amounts; valuables usually includes items made of precious metals, jewellery, furs, pictures and sculptures, collections of stamps or coins. All your valuables must not be worth more than one-third of the total you are insured for; and no individual item may be worth more than five per cent of the total
● if your home is left unoccupied for more than a month or two and you have not advised your insurers
● the first part of any claim; this 'excess' is often around £30, but can be as much as a massive £200 if you live in an area where the risk of burglary is very high
● losses of over a limited amount, often £500, from your garden.

Theft from another building (or attempted theft) of belongings, but not:
● if the building is outside the UK
● if the building is a furniture store, sale-room or exhibition room.

Damage caused by riots, mobs and political disturbances, but not:
● in Northern Ireland.

Malicious damage, for example by vandals rather than thieves, but not:
● by paying guests, tenants or 'insured persons'.

Alternative accommodation if your home is made uninhabitable, but not:
● more than 10–15 per cent of the sum you are insured for; your house buildings insurance will also provide some cover for this expense — see page 146.

Death benefit if you or your spouse die in a fire or at the hands of intruders, but only:
● up to £5,000, often as little as £1,000.

Accidental damage to some belongings, eg TVs, mirrors, glass in furniture. Many insurers offer policies with additional accidental damage cover, usually limited to belongings damaged in the home. The extra cost over a standard insured-perils-only policy is around 25 per cent.

All-risks

All-risks cover turns the standard terms and conditions of an insurance policy on its head. Instead of listing what you *are* covered for, the policy lists what you *aren't*. As well as perhaps making the policy easier to understand — if something is not definitely excluded, you can be certain you are covered — it gives extremely wide cover. For example, it gives you much more cover than insured-perils-only for belongings while they are out of your house and not in other buildings.

Some all-risks contents cover is probably essential, but it does work out more expensive. A good solution from the theft point of view is to have insured-perils-only cover on most of your belongings, and an **all-risks extension** on those that you would take out of the house — jewellery and clothes in particular. A standard all-risks extension will probably not give you extra cover for loss of money: you need yet another extra, a **money all-risks extension**, for this.

What is not covered All-risks policies will list their 'exclusions' — what they do not cover. From the theft point of view, the most important common exclusions are bicycles left unlocked in the street, contact lenses, and money over a certain limit. Like insured-perils-only policies, an all-risks policy will require you to bear the first part of any loss. This 'excess' is often around £25, but can be as high as £100. You may be offered a choice: the lower you want your excess to be, the higher the premium you'll be asked for.

House buildings insurance

House buildings insurance basically covers buildings themselves and anything fixed to them. It is unlikely that a thief will want to steal a house wall, but if he smashes a window on the way in, it is house buildings insurance that would pay for the damage. 'Buildings' includes garages, greenhouses and garden sheds; garden walls, fences, paths, drives and the like. It also pays out for alternative accommodation if your home is too badly damaged to live in. As with contents insurance, this cover is usually limited to 10–15 per cent of the sum insured — but the insured value of the building will be a lot more than the insured value of the contents, so the limit is not so restricting.

If you rent your home you may well not have any buildings insurance — mostly, it is the owner's responsibility to put right the sort of damage that buildings insurance covers. House contents insurance often includes some cover for buildings damage that your tenancy agreement makes you liable for.

Types of cover

In principle you get the same choice of policy types as with house contents insurance: indemnity or new-for-old; all-risks, insured-perils-only or standard perils plus accidental damage cover. But in practice the choice is much more straightforward.

Indemnity cover for buildings is not easy to find, and not easy to recommend. You do not have the same flexibility of settling for a second-hand replacement (or doing without a replacement altogether) as you do with house contents insurance: a broken window pane *has* to be replaced, and you cannot put up second-hand wallpaper. So new-for-old cover is almost essential. Don't be tempted to think that new-for-old cover gives you licence to neglect your property: insurers will not pay up for damage that is a result of poor maintenance.

All-risks insurance gives better cover than an insured-perils-only policy for accidental damage, but makes no difference to burglary claims.

Combined policy

Combined policies (offered through building societies) include both contents and buildings cover. You do not get any better cover than you would by buying the two types separately, but there may be an advantage when you claim — with separate policies there is sometimes confusion about which one you should claim against.

How much to insure for

Having chosen the right type of insurance policy, so that you know everything is insured against the risks you want to cover, the next stage is to insure for the right amount. If you insure for less than your goods are worth, the insurers will pay out no more than a proportion of any claim — a process known as **averaging** — and they could refuse to pay out anything at all.

Averaging works like this. Suppose you have belongings worth £10,000 (ignore, for now, what 'worth' means: it is covered below). You take out a policy giving cover of only £5,000. You have goods stolen worth £2,000. Although you have insurance cover well in excess of your claim, only half your goods were insured so you get only £1,000.

Standard policies

How much your belongings are 'worth' depends on the type of insurance you have and what you are insuring.

House contents With most house contents policies, the sum you insure for has to be the total value of all the belongings in it. Whatever kind of policy you have, antiques, jewellery and other items which are not steadily losing value must be insured for the cost of buying similar replacements. This is almost certainly a lot more than the amount you could easily sell the original items for.

For possessions that decline in value over the years, the insurance value depends on the type of policy you have.

New-for-old policies are fairly straightforward: each item has to be covered for the cost of buying a new replacement. So the correct insurance value for a five-year-old cooker is the cost of buying a similar cooker new today, and the insurance value of a three-year-old one is the same.

Indemnity insurance is more complicated: you have to work out the 'replacement value' of the goods to be insured, like this:
- ignore the original cost — unless the item is almost brand-new, it is not now relevant
- find its currrent shop price; if it is no longer made, look for the price of its nearest equivalent

• decide what its total length of life might be. This depends on the type of item: electrical goods may have a life no longer than about 10 years; a good-quality carpet perhaps 15 to 20 years; a well built table perhaps 50 years

• subtract its current age from the total length of life, and divide the figure you get by the total length of life. Multiply the result by the current price — the answer you get is the amount you should insure for. For example, suppose a new cooker similar to a five-year-old one you have lost now costs £300. You could expect a cooker to last 15 years in all, so its current replacement value is:

$$£300 \times (15 - 5) / 15 = £200$$

You have to work out insurance values for every item you possess. There is only one way to do it: go round each room of your house in turn, making a list of what you have, how you would like to insure it, and (for items to be insured under an indemnity policy), its age and life-expectancy. Then, by looking in catalogues and shop-windows, establish the current price of new equivalent goods. For some items, especially if they are worth a lot, you may want to get professional valuations (in many cases, your insurers will demand this).

Buildings House buildings insurance follows a similar philosophy: you must insure for the cost of getting back to the same position you were in before the damage. And as the damage could be the total destruction of your house (by fire, say) you must insure for the cost of completely rebuilding your house. The rebuilding cost bears no relation to the market value of a house. It is sometimes less, particularly if the house is in an area where house price rises have far outstripped building costs. But it is often more, because it must take into account the cost of clearing the site, maybe repairing adjacent houses, and other factors. Older houses, in particular, may be very expensive to restore.

It is very important to have the correct amount of buildings insurance: under-insurance could leave you very seriously out of pocket if you had to make a claim. You will need help to work out the correct rebuilding cost: for many houses, you could use the chart available from the Association of British Insurers, which helps you to calculate rebuilding costs according to the floor area, type and location of your house. If this is not appropriate for your house, you can get a professional costing from a local estate agent, chartered surveyor or valuer. Make it clear you want an estimate of rebuilding cost, not a valuation for selling. If you are just buying a house, your mortgage lender's valuer will have prepared a rebuilding valuation (the mortgage company is equally concerned to have the house correctly insured) and you should be able to rely on that.

No-calculation policies

Some policies appear to remove the need to calculate sums insured at all — but be wary of them. For example, with some buildings policies, the insurers will calculate a premium based on the details you give about your house: size, type and location. But that may cover you only up to a certain amount — which may be less than your actual rebuilding cost, and may lead to any claim you make being scaled down. Combined policies usually calculate premiums on the basis of the house rebuilding cost, and give you flat cover up to a set amount for your contents. But that cover might not be enough for all of your possessions, again leaving you under-insured.

There are some guaranteed 'no sum insured' policies for buildings: provided the information you give to the insurers is correct and complete, they promise to cover your house for its full rebuilding cost and to pay out claims in full. This is a much safer option — indeed, it is the safest. But if you want to be sure you are getting good value you still need to work out a rebuilding cost in order to determine premiums for conventional policies.

Keeping up to date

The task of valuing your possessions and buildings does not stop when you have applied for insurance. Things change from year to year, and your insurance cover must be kept up to date.

One obvious change is inflation, which increases the replacement cost of your belongings and the rebuilding cost of your house every year. Many policies are *index-linked*: the cover they give and the premium you have to pay rise automatically each year in line with inflation (usually the household goods section of the retail prices index for contents, and a special rebuilding cost index for buildings). Any rise in costs during the course of the year is also covered. With indemnity policies, index-linking is less essential when inflation is low, because you hope the rise in prices is compensated for by the lowering in value of your ageing goods. It is also less appropriate if many of your belongings change in value at a rate very different from that of the standard retail price index — antiques, say.

You can always choose a policy which is not automatically index-linked, and adjust the sum insured each year as you see fit. If you do this, you need to insure for the current value *plus* the following year's worth of inflation, so that you won't be caught out under-insured during the year.

Whichever method you choose, you also need to think about changes to your belongings and buildings over the year. You will probably buy items during the year, possibly quite large ones, and you may extend or improve your home. Add an allowance on to your cover when you renew your insurance, and tell your insurers about any major unplanned purchases as soon as you have made them.

Every few years (even with an index-linked policy) you should review your insurance cover to make sure it is up to date and does not leave you at risk.

Recording possessions The starting-point for determining how much contents insurance cover you need is a list of your possessions. Such an inventory will also be very helpful if you are burgled — and the more detailed you make it, the more helpful it can be. Both for the things you possess now and for things you buy in future, aim to record the place and date of purchase, model and serial numbers, other identifying marks, and the price you paid.

Jewellery, ornaments, and similar valuables may need more than a written description: photographs provide a far better record, both to give your insurers a clear idea of what you have lost, so that they can agree a fair settlement of your claim; and to give the police a better chance of tracing your property and identifying it as yours.

Take photographs of each item, preferably in colour, against a neutral background. It is usually suggested that you photograph one item at a time, from more than one viewpoint if necessary; make sure the photograph clearly picks up any identifying marks. Include in each picture a boldly marked ruler or a standard-sized object, such as a 50p coin, to give some idea of scale. Keep the pictures in a safe place (ideally not within your house, where they could be destroyed or stolen at the same time as the objects themselves).

If you have the necessary skill and equipment to take clear, close-up shots, do all this yourself; if not, the next best thing is to get a trusted friend to do it for you. If possible, get the pictures developed and printed privately, too — or in a shop where you don't have to give your own name and address. This may sound cloak-and-dagger stuff, and it would certainly be simpler to hand the whole job over to a professional firm (whether a general photographer, or one of the specialist firms who photograph valuables for identification). But doing so carries the risk that information about your prized possessions – perhaps even a duplicate set of prints — could get into the wrong hands.

One step up from still photographs is a video recording. You can pack more information into a video: a spoken commentary to go with each item; a rotating view of objects; mixed close-ups and long-shots to put the item into perspective. And you don't have the worry of someone else studying the pictures or keeping a copy for their own use. Despite the apparent complication, a video recording is in some ways easier to shoot than photographs — you get the results immediately, and you can experiment endlessly without extra cost. You can hire a camera-recorder by the day.

Security discounts

Perhaps surprisingly, having your home well secured does not automatically mean that your insurance will be cheaper. It is only very recently that insurers have offered security discounts at all, and they are still not universally offered.

Though discounts are important, do not place too much emphasis on them. They can amount to between 5 per cent and 25 per cent of your premium — but the difference in price between insurers, even ones offering comparable cover, can outweigh such discounts.

Different insurers treat discounts in different ways, and the market is rapidly changing. Some examples are:

• **5 per cent off** if the final exit door has a BS3621 lock, or a mortice deadlock with at least five levers, if other doors (including patio doors) are fitted to the same specification, or with key-operated bolts top and bottom, and if all accessible windows and skylights are fitted with key-operated devices; plus an **extra 5 per cent off** if you also have an NSCIA-fitted burglar alarm with a maintenance contract (but discount may not be available if the company actually requires you to have an alarm); plus an **extra 2.5 per cent off** if you are also a member of a police-approved Neighbourhood Watch scheme

• **15 per cent off** a specified make of locks

• **10–15 per cent off** if you can satisfactorily answer a detailed questionnaire about your security measures; but discount not available in inner-city areas, and your cover is void if you ever leave your house without securing all the doors and windows

• **5 per cent off** in some areas if you fit the security measures recommended by your local Crime Prevention Office

• **20 per cent off and 15 per cent no-claims discount** after one year for professional people in approved Neighbourhood Watch scheme

• **10 per cent off** if you have high-security locks on doors and windows; have lagged your pipes (burglary is not the only cause of insurance claims); and are a member of an approved Neighbourhood Watch scheme, *or* have a burglar alarm, *or* have the property occupied at least four hours a day from Monday to Friday

• **15 per cent off** if you have approved window and door locks, *and* an alarm system, plus an extra **5 per cent off** for membership of a Neighbourhood Watch scheme

• **5 per cent off** if you have an approved alarm system, plus an extra **5 per cent off** for membership of a Neighbourhood Watch

Scheme
- **25 per cent off and 15–25 per cent no-claims discount** in London area if you have approved locks and are a member of a Neighbourhood Watch Scheme
- **20 per cent off** if you have approved locks, three years' claim-free insurance, and someone at home most of the day
- **10 per cent off** if you own a dog (of any breed)
- **10 per cent off cover over £20,000** if you have 'good overall security'.

Loadings Some insurers use sticks instead of carrots: increases in premiums (called 'loadings') if your house is empty all day; if you do *not* have secure locks; if the house is a second home which is largely unoccupied; if your job is particularly 'risky'. Some may insist you take security measures as a condition of insuring you at all.

12
Dealing with a burglary

If you have followed the advice of the previous chapters, with some luck you will never need to act on the advice in this one. But no home will ever be completely burglar-proof, whatever precautions you have taken. The first part of this chapter is worth digesting now, so that you are to some extent prepared for the worst. Later sections can be consulted if and when you need them — assuming the burglar hasn't stripped your bookshelves.

Discovering a burglary

The first stage in the proceedings is that you find the evidence of a burglary, or even a burglar himself. Either you come across it (or him) on coming home; or he enters upon you, probably while you are asleep at night. Whatever the situation, and however you decide to deal with it, there is one golden rule that applies in all circumstances:

● do not tackle an intruder.

This section explains what you should do instead.

Coming home

You've been out, or away; you come home; at first, you may not even realize that you have been burgled, especially if the thief has entered through the back and you come in through the front door. But sooner or later you realize what has happened — or is happening.

The first problem is that you may not know whether the thief is still on the property; it is best to assume that he is. There is a natural temptation to announce your presence in the hope that you will scare him off without any of your belongings; but the risk in doing this is that he might attack you. The wisest course is to leave the house as quietly as possible and phone the police from a neighbouring house. Explain what you found, and tell them that you did not wait to see if the intruder was still around. While you wait for them to come, keep a watch on your house, if you can do so in safety. Play the detective, too: note down the numbers of any cars around that are unfamiliar to you.

If the thief is still in the house, he may well leave before the police arrive: if you can, note down (or try to remember) as much about him as you can: height, age, build, clothes, colour and style of hair. Did he leave in a car? Did he seem to have companions? What was he carrying? Although it will go against the grain, especially if he is carrying your belongings, it is still best not to tackle him.

The front-door burglar

If a burglar knocks at the door and forces his way in, with or without attempting to conceal his intentions, your priority must be the safety of yourself and other occupants. If you can get out of the house and escape, do so. An alternative is to lock yourself in a room which has a telephone or panic button (see page 113) and call for help.

You're there first

In some cases, especially at night, a burglar might break in expecting the house to be occupied but hoping to leave the occupants undisturbed. You won't necessarily be able to leave quickly and quietly without the burglar noticing; but if you do have that option, it is probably the best one to go for — though it may feel an unsatisfactory course at the time.

If you have a panic button, using it is a sensible alternative — the sound of an alarm will almost certainly scare a burglar away: it is too late for him to try to silence you, even if he thought it worth wasting time trying to find you. Without a panic button you are in a less strong position. A bedside telephone is worth using — if you can do so quietly: it takes time to complete even a 999 call, and a thief who hears you in the act of making a call may think it worth trying to silence you before you have had time to finish. If you can, lock your bedroom door before making the call.

Without even a telephone close by to summon help, you have two choices. One is to bury your head under the bedclothes and pretend you were mistaken about the prowler. This is probably against your instincts and may take more courage than getting up and taking action. But it may well be the wiser option, particularly if you can silently lock or bolt your bedroom door so that you cannot be reached.

The other choice is to raise the alarm within the house. You probably have the advantage that the burglar will not know how many people there are in the house, or where they are. Shout out people's names (preferably ones that sound as though they belong to large males) even if (or, indeed, especially if) you live on your own. Do this whatever your own sex, age and strength, and only then think about getting up and preparing — either for flight or fight. With any luck, the burglar will have disappeared before you have to decide which.

When you are sure you are alone, or after you have managed to leave the house, phone the police.

Telling the police

However you discover a burglar or burglary you may feel unsure of phoning the police about it: if you have gone by the book and not tackled the burglar, you probably have not seen him, and may be wondering whether you were mistaken; you may be thinking of the statistics quoted in Chapter 1, which say that the chances of catching a culprit are rare and the chances of seeing your property again are even rarer; you may think the police have better things to do, whether it's stopping potentially drunken motorists or tracking fraud in the City.

Unless you are absolutely certain that you were mistaken, and there never was an intruder, always tell the police. For a start, there is no chance of ever reducing crime unless the authorities know how much of it there is; even if involving the police brings no reward, it may prevent someone else from being burgled that evening; and if you want to claim on your insurance you almost certainly need to have informed the police of the loss.

When you phone, they will ask the appropriate questions; you in turn should find out who you have been speaking to, and where, in case you need to get back to them.

If you are in the house and staying there until the police arrive, you may well be told, in the best tradition of cops and robbers films, not to touch anything. This is important. While waiting, you may certainly *look*, but don't touch — whether with bare hand, gloves, handkerchiefs or whatever — any smooth surfaces that might bear incriminating fingerprints.

When the police arrive

Who investigates your break-in will depend on your police force's policy. It may be uniformed officers, but even a small burglary could involve CID officers and other plain-clothes police.

Your main concern will be to give them the information they want (it may well include taking the fingerprints of all members of the household; these will later be destroyed) and to find out how quickly you can put your house to rights and work out what has been taken.

Checking what's missing

The police will want a list of what has been taken — but until they give you the all-clear to tidy things up it will be difficult for you to do this. Tell them if you will be able in due course to provide detailed lists or photographs of missing things.

As you are looking through your belongings, check especially for credit cards, cheque books, building society or savings bank passbooks and so on. If any of these are missing, you should phone the companies concerned as soon as possible — straight away, at any time of the day or night, if credit or charge cards are missing (all the major companies run 24-hour answering services).

Check also for missing keys. If these are labelled they are a particular worry, and you should have the locks changed straight away; if they belong to other houses, get the police to go along there, and arrange for someone to mind the house until the owners can take control of the situation.

Make three copies of your list of missing items — one for yourself, another for the police, and the third for the insurance company (see overleaf).

Fixing damage

When the police have finished their main examination you will want to repair damage and put the place in order. This is natural, but before you go beyond immediately necessary repairs make sure your insurers know about and agree to what you propose doing — otherwise you may not be able to claim back the cost of the work; see overleaf.

Getting help

Unless you are very lucky, your burglary will have upset you — perhaps more than you realize. Relatives, friends and neighbours (particularly any that have been through the same experiences) may be a help, but many people find it easier to talk through their worries and anger with people they are not so close to. Many areas have Victims Support Schemes who can provide help and advice, and put you in touch with agencies that can provide further assistance. Get details from your police station, local Citizens Advice Bureau (CAB) or the National Association of Victims Support Schemes (NAVSS).

If you have been injured as a result of your burglary, you may be able to claim some money in compensation (whether the burglar is caught or not) through the Criminal Injuries Compensation Scheme; ask at your CAB or the NAVSS.

Claiming on your insurance

Sadly, it is often only when you make a claim on an insurance policy that you realize the importance of choosing the cover and insurer carefully — by which time, of course, it is far too late. You can help yourself by knowing how to go about claiming and what the procedure will be.

First steps

If there is damage — broken locks, smashed windows — that you must put right immediately, or if some of the missing objects need replacing without delay, phone your insurers first to make sure that you can proceed; there should be no objection. It is especially important to keep a note of the damage done, and the bills for putting it right — otherwise you may have difficulty claiming the cost back later. If there is no such urgency, let your insurers know, with a short letter or phone call, that you have had a burglary and want to make a claim.

A broker who has sold you insurance will normally help with a claim, though some will make a charge. But there is nothing to stop you dealing directly with your insurers (unless you're insured at Lloyd's, in which case you will *have* to deal with a broker, who won't charge for the work).

The claim form　Once you have registered the fact that you are going to make a claim and got the go-ahead for any urgent action, the next stage will be to fill in the claim form the insurers will send to you.

The form will ask for a list of what has been stolen or damaged, in as much detail as possible: brand, type, model numbers, when and where bought. If you have kept detailed records, this will be plain sailing; but don't be put off if you cannot supply all the details; do the best you can. You will probably be asked the price paid, but make sure you also establish and record the current shop price even if you are not asked for it, as this will be the figure you use to calculate the amount you are claiming (see page 148), which you will also be asked for.

For damaged items, send in an estimate of the repair cost; for lost items, receipts, valuations or other records such as photographs will help to establish that the item in question really did exist. Do not send originals of your documents — send copies.

Negotiating

The next stage, if the claim is a very small one and all appears to be in order, should be the arrival of a cheque. Otherwise, you are likely to get a visit from the insurers, or perhaps a **loss adjuster** hired by the insurers to check your claim.

If you are making a large claim, you may think it worthwhile appointing an expert of your own: a **loss assessor**, who will negotiate with the insurers or their loss adjuster on your behalf, in return for a fee (about 10 per cent on a claim of up to, say, £5,000). If you are going to these lengths, it would be best to get the assessor involved at the beginning to help fill in your claim form: they are skilled not only in making sure your claim is largely met by the insurers, but also in making sure you claim all that you are entitled to.

However the claim is handled, you will in due course get an offer of payment from your insurers. If this is close to what you wanted or expected, you can accept it; if not, try negotiating further. Even when you do accept an offer, you need to leave yourself room to go back later with another claim if, for example, you later find other items are missing or have been damaged. So don't sign a payment notice 'in full and final settlement' of the claim without adding a rider to that effect.

Problems Disputes may arise when you claim on your insurance. Your ideas of what you are insured for and how much your belongings are worth may be different from your insurers'. If persistent negotiation or the services of a loss assessor don't produce a satisfactory result, you may be able to take your case up with one of the two services which have been set up to help resolve such difficulties.

The larger one is the **The Insurance Ombudsman Bureau** (IOB); but some insurers take part instead in the **Personal Insurance Arbitration Service** (PIAS). You can take advantage of these schemes only if:

- your insurers are in the scheme
- your policy qualifies (for example, the Insurance Ombudsman cannot deal with certain issues, such as third-party claims)
- you have reached deadlock with your insurers (after reference to a senior official)
- you make your appeal promptly — for a claim to the Ombudsman, within six months of your final failure to agree.

You can make use of the Ombudsman scheme without the

agreement of your insurer — once you have reached a stale-mate, simply write to the company's Chief Executive giving three week's notice of your intention to approach the Ombuds-man. The PIAS scheme requires the agreement of the insurers.

The schemes have other differences, too. The Ombudsman's decision is binding on the insurers, but not on you (so, if appropriate, you could then take legal action); the PIAS decision is binding on both of you. The Ombudsman can award up to £100,000; PIAS is usually limited to £25,000.

If you are insured through Lloyd's, their Consumer Enquir-ies Department is your first port of call. Lloyd's are planning to join the IOB.

13
Further information

Having read through the last 150 pages, you will now have a good understanding of how to make your home secure. What's next? You will need to buy security products; talk to security experts; evaluate how much it all might cost.

That's where this chapter will help you. It lists names and addresses of suppliers and organizations; prices of typical hardware; people to contact for further advice.

For each of the chapters, you will find headings dealing with:

• **prices** for the main types of hardware. Prices obviously vary widely, so the ones listed here can be only a general idea of what you might have to pay. They are correct for October 1987

• **suppliers** of the hardware mentioned. This cannot be a definitive list: firms and equipment come and go. But it will give you a starting point. Firms and equipment listed have not been tested in any way – so exclusion does not imply disapproval, any more than inclusion indicates a recommendation, or even an indication of suitability for any task. The lists generally do not include firms that will supply equipment only if they also install it themselves

• **tricky to find** hardware: names of suppliers of individual kinds of equipment mentioned in the text which you won't find in every do-it-yourself or lock shop.

Then follows a list of the organizations mentioned in those chapters; and general security trade organizations who can offer you advice and information in varying degrees.

Chapter 3:
Making appearances deceptive

Prices

Proximity detector £65
Automatic light switch
– photoelectric-operated £13
– photoelectric/on, timer/off £15

Suppliers

C-Tec
Hoover
Litton
Meadroy
Pifco
Polycell
Smiths
Superswitch

Tricky to find

Proximity detector C-Tec; Hoover; Litton; Meadroy; Smiths; Superswitch

Chapter 5: Doors and door locks

Prices

Door chain £4
– lockable £20
Door check £5
Door viewer £4
Personal attack alarm £7
Video camera door system £400
Security door and frame from £400
Five-lever mortice lock to BS3621 £20 to £80
Cylinder rim lock, automatically deadlocking £30
Locks keyed to pass, key registration service £2 to £5; often no extra cost, though mainly on higher-priced locks

Flush-mounted bolts £6
Patio door locks £10
Mortice rack bolt £5
Dog (hinge) bolt £4 a pair
Surface-mounted locking bolt £5

Suppliers

Abloy
Ademco
Berol
Bramah
Burt Bolton
C-Tec
Chubb
Churchill
ERA
Fichet
Hoover
Houseguard
Ingersoll
Kaba
Legge
Pifco
Polycell
Raytel
Squire
Union
Yale

Non-locking hardware (eg tower and barrel bolts; flush-mounted bolts) is often unbranded. Try builder's merchants, ironmongers, and 'architectural ironmongery' suppliers.

Tricky to find

Lockable door chain Hoover
Door check Chubb; Ingersoll
Security door Burt Bolton; Fichet
Key registration service Abloy; Bramah; Ingersoll; Kaba

Chapter 6: Windows and window locks

Prices

Glazing, per square metre, includes cutting costs. (Ordinary 4mm window glass is £10 a square metre.)
– toughened £23
– laminated £39
– Georgian wired £17
– polycarbonate £42
– polystyrene £18
Window bolt, automatically locking £5
Hinged staple bolt £5
Mortice rack bolt £4
Locking cockspur handle £8
Locking fitch catch £5
Cockspur lock, key operated £4
Casement stay lock £2
Sliding sash dual-screw fitting £2

Suppliers

Chubb
ERA
Ingersoll
Kaba
Legge
Louvre Lock Co
Polycell
Rola
Squire
Union
Yale

Glass of all types should be available from local glass merchants. Similarly, plastics suppliers will provide polycarbonate and cheaper transparent plastics; or look for advertisments of suppliers in do-it-yourself magazines.

Tricky to find

Louvre window lock Louvre Lock Co

Hinged staple lock Chubb; Polycell; Yale
Locking cockspur handle ERA; Kaba; Polycell; Union; Yale
Locking fitch catch Polycell
Casement stay lock, key operated ERA; Kaba; Union

Chapter 7: Garden security

Prices

Electric up-and-over garage door opener £325
Lock for up-and-over garage door, high-security £42
Padbolt, about 200mm long £3
Hasp and staple, about 200mm long £4
Security locking bar £15 to £50
Minimum five-lever/cylinder padlock £12 to £48
Close-shackle five-lever/cylinder padlock £27 to £74
Padlock keyed to pass with house doors often no extra cost,
though found more often on the higher-priced locks
Lockable ladder brackets £15 a pair
Anti-climb paint £10 for 2½ litres

Suppliers

Abloy
Aldridge
Apex
Bramah
Chubb
ERA
Fichet
Ingersoll
Kaba
Legge
Squire
Stanley
Thunder Screw Anchors
Union
Wailes
Yale

Tricky to find

Electric garage door opener Apex; Stanley
Lock for up-and-over garage door, high-security Abloy; Kaba
Security locking bar Chubb; ERA; Ingersoll; Squire; Yale
Lockable ladder brackets Thunder Screw Anchors
Anti-climb paint Aldridge; Wailes

Chapter 8: Alarm systems

Prices

Do-it-yourself kit £150
Professionally installed system to NSCIA £700
Auto-dialler from £120
Detectors
– simple magnetic contacts, pressure mats etc £1.50 to £4
– infra-red, or ultrasonic, movement detector £40
– microwave movement detector £115
Dummy bell box £15
Shunt switch £10
Wireless signalling *extra* cost £550

Suppliers

Ademco
Advanced Design Electronics
Advanced Security Products
Blade
C-TEC
Cameo of London
Castle Alarms
Hoover
Houseguard
J Harvey Systems
Superswitch
Tunstall Security

Tricky to find

Components Many of the firms listed make or distribute, or could get, almost any burglar alarm component you wanted: try especially Ademco; Advanced Security Products; C-TEC; Castle Alarms; Houseguard; J Harvey Systems
Shunt switch For a switch built into a door lock, try firms above, or Kaba
Wireless signalling Superswitch

Chapter 9: Security for valuables

Prices

Domestic safe
– wall-mounted £115
– floor-mounted £200
Hobbyist's engraving equipment £10
Invisible security marking kit £2
Bank vaults etc
– envelope £6 a year
– boxes, depending on size £14 to £25 a year
– access fee £5 a visit
(above fees may be waived under some 'free banking' deals)
– safety deposit centre anything from £35 to £550 a year depending on location, size etc

Suppliers

Berol
Bramah
Chubb
Churchill
Fichet
Hamber Safes
Hoover
Polycell
Securikey
Swiss Glass Engraving

170 Protecting your home

Chapter 10: Fire safety

Prices

Fire blanket to BS6575 £22
Fire extinguisher, multi-purpose powder to BS5423 £25
Smoke alarm
– independent unit £10 to £20: price depends more on brand
than on features (eg type of detector, with or without light etc)
– detector for burglar alarm system £20

Suppliers

Ademco
Black & Decker
C-Tec
Chubb
Fichet
First Alert
Hoover
Houseguard
Pifco
Polycell
Rentokil
Thorn Security
Tutor

Tricky to find

Fire blanket to BS6575 Chubb; Rentokil; Tutor
Smoke detector
– for burglar alarm system C-Tec
– combined ionization/photoelectric Pifco

Chapter 11: Insurance

There are literally dozens of insurers, and hundreds of insurance brokers — far too many to list here. The head office of the sponsors of this book is:

Norwich Union Fire Insurance Society Ltd
Surrey Street
Norwich
NR1 3TA
✆(0603) 622200

Prices

The cost of **contents insurance** depends as much on where you live as on the type of insurance you want. The two rates in each category below are first for a country area and then for very high-risk inner-city area. They are the rates for each £1,000 of goods insured. Remember that with new-for-old cover you insure your goods for a higher value than with indemnity.

Insured-perils-only, indemnity £2 to £7
Insured-perils-only, new-for-old £3.50 to £10
All-risks, new-for-old £6 to £13
– but valuables and things you take out of the house are often charged at £14 to £30

House buildings insurance does not usually depend on where you live. A typical rate per £1,000 of cover is:
Insured-perils-only, new-for-old £1.50

Addresses

Suppliers

Abloy Locking Devices Ltd
3 Hatters Lane
Croxley Centre
Watford
Hertfordshire
WD1 8YY
✆(0923) 55066

Ademco Distribution Ltd
Unit 5 Cutbush Park
Lower Earley
Reading
Berkshire
RG6 4UT
✆(0734) 868641

Advanced Design Electronics
see Advanced Security Products

Advanced Security Products Ltd
Ealing Road
Aintree
Liverpool
L9 0HU
✆051-523 8440

Aldridge
see Angel Lock and Safe Co

Angel Lock and Safe Co
337 Goswell Road
London
EC1 7JH
✆01-837 8506

Apex Doors Ltd
Crown Lane
Horwich
Bolton
Lancashire
BL6 5HP
✆(0204) 68151

BRK Electronics
see First Alert

Berol Ltd
Oldmeadow Road
King's Lynn
Norfolk
PE30 4JR
✆(0553) 761221

Black & Decker
West Point
The Grove
Slough
Berkshire
SL1 1QQ
✆(0753) 74277

Blade Electronic Security
see Advanced Security Products

Bramah Security Equipment Ltd
31 Oldbury Place
London
W1M 3AP
✆01-935 7148

Burt Bolton Architectural Co
Burts Wharf
Crabtree Manorway
Belvedere
Kent
DA17 6BD
✆01-311 5100

C-TEC Security
Stephen's Way
Goose Green
Wigan
Lancashire
WN3 6PH
✆(0942) 322744

Cameo of London
38 Woodland Road
London
E4 7EU
✆01-524 8425

Castle Alarms
North Street
Winkfield
Berkshire
SL4 4SY
✆(0344) 886446

Chubb Lock Company
PO Box 197
Wednesfield Road
Wolverhampton
WV10 0ET
✆(0902) 55111

Chubb Safe Equipment Company
PO Box 61
Wednesfield Road
Wolverhampton
WV10 0EW
⌀(0902) 55111

Churchill Safes & Security Products
Brymbo Road Industrial Estate
Holditch
Newcastle-under-Lyme
Staffordshire
ST5 9HX
⌀(0782) 621003

ERA
see J E Reynolds

Fichet UK Ltd
22-24 Marlborough Grove
London
SE1 5JT
⌀01-231 1137

First Alert
12 The Paddock
Hambridge Road
Newbury
Berkshire
RG14 5TQ
⌀(0635) 38836

Hamber Safes
Hamber & Whiskin Engineering
Radford Way
Billericay
Essex
CM12 0AG
⌀(0277) 624450

Henry Squire and Sons
New Invention
Short Heath
Willenhall
West Midlands
WV12 5BD
✆(0922) 476711

Hoover Security
Avenue 2
Station Lane Industrial Estate
Witney
Oxfordshire
OX8 6JE
✆(0993) 71337

Houseguard Security Wholesalers Ltd
Highland House
Longman Road
Inverness
IV1 1RY
✆(0463) 230995

Industrial Devices Ltd
309 West End Lane
London
NW6 1RG
✆01-431 1118

Ingersoll Locks Ltd
Forsyth Road
Sheerwater
Woking
Surrey
GU21 5RS
✆(04862) 23551

J E Reynolds & Co
Era Works
Straight Road
Short Heath
Willenhall
West Midlands
WV12 5RA
∅(0922) 401515

J Harvey Systems (Alarms)
FREEPOST (BS4 500)
Avonmouth
Bristol
BS11 0BR
∅(0272) 621549

J Legge & Co Ltd
Moat Street
Willenhall
West Midlands
WV13 1TD
∅(0902) 366332

Kaba Locks Ltd
Woodward Road
Howden Industrial Estate
Tiverton
Devon
EX16 5HW
∅(0884) 256464

Legge
see J Legge & Co

Litton Security Products
6 First Avenue
Globe Park
Marlow
Buckinghamshire
SL7 1YA
⌀(06284) 6060

Locks Ltd
31 Oldbury Place
Marylebone High Street
London
W1M 3AP
⌀01-935 7147

Louvre Lock Co
118 Stockwell Road
London
SW9 9HR
⌀01-737 0100

Markitwise International
Maylite Trading Estate
Martley
Worcestershire
WR6 6PQ
⌀(08866) 226

Meadroy Ltd
88 High Road
South Benfleet
Essex
SS7 5LN
⌀(0268) 794035

Norwich Union
see page 170

Pifco Ltd
Failsworth
Manchester
M35 0HS
✆061-681 8321

Polycell Products Ltd
Broadwater Road
Welwyn Garden City
Hertfordshire
AL7 3AZ
✆(0707) 328131

Raytel Security Systems Ltd
Raytel House
Brook Road
Rayleigh
Essex
SS6 7XH
✆(0268) 775656

Rola
see Locks Ltd

Rentokil
see Tutor (at the time of going to press, it was expected that
Tutor would start packaging a fire blanket for Rentokil)

Securikey Ltd
PO Box 18
Aldershot
Hampshire
GU12 4SL
✆(0252) 3118889

Smiths Industries Environmental Controls Company Ltd
Waterloo Road
Cricklewood
London
NW2 7UR
✆01-450 8944

Squire
see Henry Squire & Sons

Stanley Automatic Openers
UK Distributors:
Cardale Doors Ltd
Buckingham Road Industrial Estate
Brackley
Northamptonshire
NN13 5EA
✆(0280) 703022

Superswitch Electric Appliances Ltd
Houldsworth Street
Reddish
Stockport
Cheshire
SK5 6BZ
✆061-431 4885

Swiss Glass Engraving
see Markitwise International

Thorn Security Ltd
Security House
Grosvenor Road
Twickenham
Middlesex
TW1 4AB
✆01-892 4422

Thunder Screw Anchors
Victoria Way
Burgess Hill
West Sussex
∅(04446) 5701

Tunstall Security Ltd
Hither Green
Clevedon
Avon
BS21 6XU
∅(0272) 870078

Tutor Safety Products
Sturminster Newton
Dorset
DT10 1BZ
∅(0258) 73181

Union Locks Limited
PO Box 15
Willenhall
West Midlands
WV13 1JS
∅(0902) 634136

Wailes Dove Bitumastic plc
Hedgeley Road
Hebburn
Tyne & Wear
NE31 1EY
∅091-483 2321

Yale Security Products Ltd
Wood Street
Willenhall
West Midlands
WV13 1LA
∅(0902) 366911

Organizations

ABI
Association of British Insurers
Aldermary House
10-15 Queen Street
London
EC4N 1TT
✆01-248 4477

BAFE
British Approvals for Fire Equipment
48a Eden Street
Kingston-upon-Thames
Surrey
KT1 1EE
✆01-541 1950

BIBA
British Insurance Brokers Association
BIBA House
14 Bevis Marks
London
EC3A 7NT
✆01-623 9043

BSI
British Standards Institution
2 Park Street
London
W1A 2BS
✆01-629 9000

BSIA
British Security Industry Association
Witco House
Barbourne Road
Worcester
WR1 1RT
✆(0905) 21464

CAB
Citizens Advice Bureau
Local CABs are listed in the front of your phone book, under
'Useful numbers' in the Local Information section.

CORGI
Confederation for the Registration of Gas Installers
St Martin's House
140 Tottenham Court Road
London
W1P 9LN
✆01-387 9185

Criminal Injuries Compensation Board
Whittington House
19 Alfred Place
London
WC1E 7LG
✆01-636 9501

GGF
Glass & Glazing Federation
44-48 Borough High Street
London
SE1 1XB
✆01-403 7177

IAAI
Inspectors Approved Alarms Installers
2 Commercial Road
South Gosforth
Newcastle-upon-Tyne
NE3 1QJ
☎091-285 7591

Institute of Public Loss Assessors
14 Red Lion Street
Chesham
Buckinghamshire
HP5 1HB
☎(0494) 782342

IOB
Insurance Ombudsman Bureau
31 Southampton Row
London
WC1B 5HJ
☎01-242 8613

Lloyd's
Consumer Enquiries Department
London House
6 London Street
London
EC3R 7AB
☎01-623 7100

NICEIC
National Inspection Council for Electrical Installations
Contracting
Vintage House
36-37 Albert Embankment
London
SE1 7UJ
☎01-582 7746

NSCIA
National Supervisory Council for Intruder Alarms
Queensgate House
14 Cookham Road
Maidenhead
Berkshire
SL6 8AJ
✆(0628) 37512

NAVSS
National Association of Victims Support Schemes
17a Electric Lane
Brixton
London
SW9 8LA
✆01-326 1984

PIAS
Personal Insurance Arbitration Service
The Chartered Institute of Arbitrators
75 Cannon Street
London
EC4N 5BH
✆01-236 8761

Security Lock Association
Penfold House
Brent Street
London
NW4 2EU
✆01-202 7821

Index